Working with Elderly People

Working with Elderly People

A Care Worker's Handbook

A. Murphy

Matador
9 Priory Business Park,
Wistow Road, Kibworth Beauchamp,
Leicestershire. LE8 0RX
Tel: (+44) 116 279 2299
Fax: (+44) 116 279 2277
Email: books@troubador.co.uk
Web: www.troubador.co.uk/matador

ISBN 978 1784620 523

British Library Cataloguing in Publication Data.
A catalogue record for this book is available from the British Library.

Printed and bound in the UK by TJ International, Padstow, Cornwall
Typeset in 11pt Aldine401 BT Roman by Troubador Publishing Ltd, Leicester, UK

Matador is an imprint of Troubador Publishing Ltd

CONTENTS

DISCLAIMER

Every care has been taken when compiling these notes, but the writers cannot be held responsible for any omissions or errors of fact in the information included.

The writers also regret that they cannot accept any responsibility for any incidents, accidents, injuries or other damages to persons or property arising from the use of information, procedures, aids or equipment mentioned in this book.

ACKNOWLEDGEMENTS

I should like to thank the following people who have helped to make this book possible:

Jean Allen, Continence Advisory Service, Community Health, Sheffield.
Elizabeth Highfield, formerly Chief Audiology Technician, Royal Hallamshire Hospital, Sheffield.
Janet Hogger, Community Physiotherapist, Community Health, Sheffield.
Isobel O'Leary, Senior Speech and Language Therapist, Community Health, Sheffield.
Kevin Price, formerly Mobility Officer for the Blind, Social Services, Sheffield.
and also other staff who have read this book.

I am also grateful to the following for permission to use copyright illustrations:

Handicapped Living Centre, Sheffield, for drawings of walking aids and a table; Academic Press for drawings of a walking frame in use from *An Outline of Geriatrics* by H.M. Hodgkinson; Churchill Livingstone for drawings of going up and down stairs and fitting and propelling a wheelchair from *The Practice of Occupational Therapy* by Ann Turner; Everest & Jennings Inc. for drawings showing how to negotiate stairs with a wheelchair from their booklet *Wheelchair Owner's Manual*; The Disability Information Trust for 14 drawings on using a wheelchair from *Wheelchairs* (5th edition); The Department of Health for a drawing of a wheelchair footplate from *Hints on the Use of Your Wheelchair;* J & P. Coats for drawings of crochet and embroidery stitches from their booklets; Boxtree for three drawings of a bottle garden from *Gardening Time* by William Davidson (Tiger Books); Horticultural Therapy for five drawings from *Able to Garden* by P. Please (Batsford); Age Concern for three drawings from *Gardening in Retirement* by Isobel Pays and the Community Transport Association for information on their training courses.

Finally, I should like to thank RADAR for allowing me to use the chart reproduced on p.46 from their book *Choosing a Wheelchair*.

PREFACE

Staff working in day centres, residential homes and other units for elderly people have often expressed a need for a book that brings together helpful information and ideas. This collection of notes was compiled while working in a day centre with elderly people who had a range of different physical conditions. It was originally prepared for new staff who were starting to work in the centre for the first time and was intended as a simple introduction to some of the activities that could be used there.

It also seemed a good idea to provide information about the running of the centre and the elderly people who use it. When working with people who may be frail or have a disability, staff need to know how to look after them, help them to cope with their disabilities and be able to take action in an emergency.

The second part of the book covers different kinds of activities. These are meant to provide interest, entertainment and mental stimulation. Most of them can be done quite easily in a centre and many are pastimes and hobbies which the elderly people may choose to do for themselves.

In the Appendices there are suggestions for further sources of information such as books, addresses of suppliers and organisations concerned with elderly people.

I hope that you will find the notes helpful and of benefit and that they may be useful in giving you ideas about other activities.

A.M.

PART ONE

BASIC INFORMATION

1

PART ONE

BASIC INFORMATION

1 CENTRES, STAFF AND CLIENTS

In this book the word 'centre' has been used to mean anywhere where elderly people may meet together – a group run by volunteers, a luncheon club, a day centre, a residential home, nursing home or other long-stay unit.

A day centre is a place where they can go for a few hours during the day to enjoy social or recreational activities, whether for one day a week or more often, either on a weekday or at the weekend. The centre may be used by people who have a mental or physical disability or special needs, or simply by those who would benefit from company, a meal, bathing, hairdressing, counselling, advice or any other support. Carers may also appreciate having respite from an elderly relative. Other services, which may be available, could include nursing, chiropody, social work, and physiotherapy, occupational therapy and so on.

Day centres may be managed by a Local Authority, voluntary organisation or by a private concern, or they may be run by volunteers from a local charity, church or community group. They may be held in a community centre or church hall, in adapted premises or in a specially built centre, or they may be part of a residential home or other unit.

The type of staff in the centre will depend on the organisation that is responsible for running it. If it is managed by a Local Authority or an institution there could be paid staff who have had training and experience in providing the different services; if it is run by a local voluntary group the services offered maybe more limited.

The atmosphere should be as happy and relaxed as possible, so that the elderly people can feel free to enjoy themselves and take part in any of the activities which may be available. These should be suited to the abilities of those who attend and should also be of benefit to them, providing interest and stimulation.

In some centres the elderly people who go there may not be mobile or may live some distance away, so that transport will have to be arranged. This may be by ambulance or an adapted vehicle (one which will take wheelchairs), or taxis and cars can be used if people can manage these easily. In some areas special transport schemes for elderly and disabled people maybe available, or 'friends' of the centre may have contributed towards a minibus, which may be shared with other centres.

From time to time it will be necessary to check how the centre is running and whether it is keeping up with its aims, and to ensure that the people who attend are benefiting from being there, and able to take part in activities which they have chosen.

THE LAYOUT OF A CENTRE

If a centre is to be used by people with a physical disability, it may need to be adapted so that it will be safe and suitable for them. This could mean providing level access from the road, doorways and fire exits that are wide enough to take the widest wheelchair (with a person propelling it himself) that is a width of 900mm or more when the door is open. Handrails in convenient places such as on door jambs, along corridors, beside steps and in toilet and bathing areas, and also enough space for someone to turn and use a wheelchair in a confined space like a toilet. If there are people with a visual impairment who walk unaided, it may be necessary to provide continuous handrails around the centre.

Furniture and fittings also need to be appropriate for the people who attend, and in a centre for elderly people these could include a selection of armchairs at different heights. Vinyl coverings on chairs help to protect them from damage or stains, and sometimes additional cushions or supports can be added to make the sitter more comfortable or secure. If stacking chairs are used these may also need to have armrests. Footstools are used in some centres.

Tables should be suitable for the particular activities – for example, occasional tables can be used for reading magazines, while worktables should be at a convenient height for the people using them, whether they are standing or sitting down in a chair or wheelchair. Sometimes tables have to be stackable if space is limited.

Floors must be safe to walk on, and non-slip floor coverings or fitted short-pile carpets will help to prevent people from falling, although coverings on which the feet tend to 'stick' may be hazardous. If drinks, food or urine are likely to be spilt on the floor, Flotex carpets or surfaces that are easy to clean will have to be used.

If a centre is on more than one level it may be necessary to install a ramp (minimum 1 in 12) or a lift or stairlift to provide access to another storey, but ordinary stairs may be adequate if the elderly people are agile enough to use them.

In areas where people may fall easily, such as toilets, alarms may be needed, and also outward-opening or sliding doors and locks that can be operated from the outside. Additional aids such as raised toilet seats and free-standing toilet frames can be added later, and hoists and commode chairs which fit over toilets can be made available if these are needed.

Wheelchairs, walking aids and other equipment can be kept in a storage area when not in use; this may need to be locked at night if the centre is also used by other groups for different purposes.

Other facilities, which may be needed, include a dining room, a lounge/TV room, a games room, quiet/rest room, chiropody and treatment room, bathroom, hairdressing area and places for other activities. The outside of the building must allow easy access for people who are both elderly and disabled from either ambulances or public transport, and seats should be provided inside and outside for those who are only able to walk short distances.

If a building has very narrow corridors that do not allow wheelchairs to be manoeuvred, or would require major adaptations such as the installation of a lift, it would be worthwhile looking for different premises, which are easier to use.

PROVIDING CARE

As we have seen, a centre designed for elderly people must be safe, easy to use and accessible. Good lighting is also essential, as well as adequate ventilation and enough heating to ensure that the room temperature is comfortable for people who are likely to be sitting down for most of the day. In a day room the temperature should be over 21°C (70°F) and in a bedroom no lower than 12°C (54°F)

The elderly people may need to be encouraged to use the furniture and equipment that is most suited to their particular needs – for example, a chair of the right height and size, or a table which is at a convenient working height for any given activity. If a person needs a cushion, staff will need to find out which is the most appropriate one to use. The local occupational therapist, Disabled Living Centre or District Health Authority should be able to advise about this, and it may be worthwhile having a selection of different cushions in the centre, so that clients can try them out and choose the one they prefer. Some people may also want a rug, footstool, incontinence cover and so on.

Many elderly people are able to look after themselves without any assistance, while others may depend on staff for quite a lot of their needs. Despite this, they should be encouraged to be as independent as possible while engaged in activities that they can do safely.

In any centre, it is helpful if members of staff can work together as a team. This not only improves their efficiency but also benefits the service being provided and helps staff to feel that they are making a real contribution to the running of the centre. Staff meetings can also be used as a means of raising issues and discussing problems and progress.

Any centre must follow the Health and Safety regulations so that staff, elderly people and any visitors are not at risk. These will probably have been drawn up by the organisation responsible for the running of the centre and should be kept in a place where all staff can read them. In a centre run by volunteers there may be no existing regulations, and a set of appropriate guidelines will need to be obtained (the local Social Services Department may be able to help).

VOLUNTARY WORKERS

Volunteers can contribute a great deal to a centre – by assisting the staff and elderly people, or by doing tasks around the unit. This will improve the service and also enable the staff to provide additional activities.

Staff need to be careful when accepting volunteers and should check that they are suitable for work in a centre with elderly people. This may mean using the same procedures as with the paid staff – filling in an application form (with the names of two people willing to give a reference) and attending for an interview. This is important, particularly if the volunteer is going to drive, handle money or be alone with the elderly people.

The application form can be quite simple (see p. 7) and the interview informal, but staff need to know whether the person is in good health mentally and physically, and whether she will be able to undertake whatever work she may be asked to do. She should also be genuinely interested in elderly people and be able to communicate and work with them. During the interview she may ask to look round the centre, meet the elderly people and see what kind of activities she will be doing. She may enquire about supervision and training, and also about the reimbursement of expenses.

When taking on volunteers it is important to review the Health and Safety provisions and to find out whether the volunteer and centre are covered by insurance. This may be needed if the volunteer is involved in an accident and should cover all contingencies – her own fault or someone else's, injury to herself, an elderly person, a member of staff or the general public, and loss or damage to property. Accidents can happen in many different ways. A minibus or piece of equipment may be poorly maintained or faulty; the volunteer may have had insufficient supervision or training, or an elderly person may be awkward to manage. Volunteer drivers should find out whether their motor insurance covers the work for the centre – some insurance companies will provide this cover at no extra cost.

To avoid an accident happening, staff must follow the Health and Safety policy of the centre and be aware of any guidelines when dealing with volunteers. These should include ensuring that they are capable of doing all the activities required of them, providing adequate supervision and training and checking that the volunteer knows

VOLUNTARY SERVICES

Dear.......................   Date........................

Thank you for offering to visit our centre as a volunteer. We need to provide information about our volunteers and it would be appreciated if you could let us have the following details about yourself.

Name:
Address:

Telephone No.:   Date of birth:_/_/_

Have you any experience with the elderly or special skills or interests?

Can you give the names of two people who would be willing to give you a reference?

Would you like to help with any of these activities? (please tick)

□ reading to the elderly	□ helping with outings
□ talking to the elderly	□ film or slide shows
□ helping the staff	□ concerts
□ refreshments	□ sing-songs
□ fundraising	□ playing the piano
□ helping with events	□ music
□ games	□ socials or parties
□ craftwork	□ outdoor activities
□ gardening	□ other activities:
□ driving the minibus	

Are there any particular days or times which are most convenient to you?

I hope that you will enjoy coming to our centre,

Yours sincerely,
Manager, Broadlands Centre
Please return to the Voluntary Services Co-ordinator, Social Services Dept.

where her responsibility ends. The volunteer should know who is supervising her, and whom to contact for support, information and training. This may be a Voluntary Services Co-ordinator or a member of staff in the centre.

A fund should be maintained to pay the expenses of any volunteers who may be out of pocket through visiting the centre.

ELDERLY PEOPLE

A person is usually regarded as 'elderly' when he or she has reached retirement age, although how someone performs mentally or physically will vary from one individual to another – some are quite young at 70 while others are 'old' at a much younger age. This may cause problems in a day centre when staff have to try and decide who should attend: some centres will only accept people up to the age of 60 or 65, while others will not take people under retirement age.

As people grow older they may no longer be able to take part in activities which they could do previously; this may be due to failing eyesight, reduced hearing, forgetfulness, limited concentration, anxiety, confusion, loss of confidence or interest, or because they have a particular complaint that affects their ability to perform a task, such as pain, stiffness, deformity, immobility, weakness, discomfort, breathlessness, depression and so on (see Appendices for list of conditions).

Older people may also be affected by events and circumstances such as bereavement, isolation, poor home conditions, restricted environment, altered home circumstances, poverty, poor diet, loss of independence, constant admissions to hospital, lack of support from family and friends, and perhaps also lack of support and advice from Health and Social Services.

How a person copes with the different situations may depend upon his or her previous attitudes and expectations – some people may be able to accept change while others may become aggressive, agitated, unco-operative, withdrawn or depressed.

Sometimes an elderly person has to decide whether to move into a long-stay unit and this can be a difficult time, often associated with the death of a partner, sudden disability, deteriorating mental or physical condition, or simply because a carer or support services are no longer able to cope with the situation. When the decision has been made, the elderly person has to adjust to the loss of his or her own home and become familiar with new surroundings, people and routines. It may mean having to adapt to some loss of privacy and learning to live with other people.

Staff need to be aware of any difficulties that the elderly person may be experiencing, so that they can give support and encouragement and provide help in overcoming them.

INTERVIEWING CLIENTS

How an elderly person is approached on his or her first day can be very important. Those who have never heard of or attended a centre before may feel quite shy and nervous and could easily be upset by being addressed rather sharply or abruptly. Initially, nothing more than a general introduction will be needed, but later it may be necessary to ask a few simple questions, particularly if very little is known about the person – name, address, date of birth, condition, any medication and details about the client's doctor, social worker and next of kin. If the next of kin is a relative living some distance away, it maybe useful to have a note about friends and neighbours living locally, and their whereabouts during the day and at night.

If the elderly person seems a little overwhelmed, it may be a good idea to suggest that you would like to ask him some simple questions later on, so that he is prepared. Sometimes you may be asked why the questions have to be answered, and it will help to have some short answer ready.

Information from interviews will need to be written down later in a client's file or notes and any other details added when necessary. It is important for essential notes to be quickly and easily read! Try to avoid writing too much in front of the person you are questioning, although you may have to jot down a few brief notes.

When asking about a person and his condition, you should find out all that will affect your care and treatment of him while he is attending the centre, but irrelevant questions should be avoided. In some centres, staff may be able to get information from a doctor, social worker or another member of staff, but in other instances it may be necessary to question the person himself. Staff need to be aware that an elderly person's account of his own condition and medication is not always accurate or reliable and that they may still have to contact a doctor if they have any queries. Details about medication are important, particularly if a person has to take this during his stay in the centre. Elderly people with conditions such as diabetes, epilepsy or heart and chest complaints may need special attention from the staff. Other information you may need could include special diets, need for regular toileting and any special procedures, arrangements or aids which the person may need to use.

Interests, hobbies and past occupations are a useful guide for any member of staff who is responsible for organising activities and encouraging the elderly people to take part in them, and it enables her to ask them what they would like to do.

If the centre is not a residential one, staff will also need to make arrangements for transporting the person to and from the centre and also for contacting any relations or neighbours if a person is unable to attend. These points should be raised during your interview.

SOCIAL SERVICES DEPARTMENT
DAY CENTRES

Centre	Date
Name: Address: Tel No:	Date of birth
	Case number
	Marital state
Next of Kin or person to be contacted in emergency Name: Address: Tel No:	Social Worker Welfare Assistant Area
	GP Address Tel No
Disability	
Any special medication or precautions	
Past employment	
Interests or Hobbies	
Notes	
This client is to attend the _____ centre on _____ days and will travel by _____ transport. He/she started at the centre on _____ and is non/ambulent. <div style="text-align:right">Notes overleaf</div>	

When interviewing an elderly person it is important to pick a suitable time and place so that he or she feels relaxed and is able to talk freely. Any personal information disclosed during the interview should be confidential to the staff who need to know it and should be kept in a place where it cannot be seen by others attending the centre.

A sample of a typical referral or interview form is given on the previous page.

SOME CONDITIONS

ARTHRITIS

Arthritis is a condition which affects the joints causing inflammation and pain. It covers different conditions, the two most common ones are Rheumatoid Arthritis and Osteoarthritis.

Rheumatoid Arthritis

In this condition the main symptoms are pain and swelling in the joints and there can also be stiffness and deformity. The joints usually affected are the shoulders, hands, wrists, knees and feet though it may be found in the neck, elbows and hips. It often affects women between the ages of 40 – 50 though it can occur at any age.

Treatment is usually by drugs and therapy – this can be exercises, advice on joint protection, splints and easier ways of doing things around the home. A person can help himself by having rests in between exercise, protecting his own joints, eating a well balanced diet and keeping to a normal weight.

Osteoarthritis

In Osteoarthritis the surfaces inside the joints become damaged and this can lead to pain, stiffness, swelling and a feeling of 'grating' when the joints move. The parts of the body most likely to be affected are the neck, back, hips, hands and knees. To relieve the condition a person may be given exercises, painkillers and be encouraged not to put too much pressure on the joints – sometimes there may be a need for surgery to replace the joints if the condition is severe.

In a centre the person needs to be able to sit comfortably in a supporting chair of the right height and have a table which is convenient nearby.

Activities need to be suitable for him and not put any strain on the joints or be too repetitive. Often it may be easier to adapt activities so that they are easier to do or it maybe possible to use aids or other equipment.

Sometimes people may need to be shown how to 'pace' themselves so that they don't overdo activities or perhaps do too little – they also have to learn how to rest in between activities.

Note: Arthritis Research UK have a selection of booklets on the different aspects of Arthritis, these are available from Arthritis Research UK, Copeman House, St. Mary's Court, St Mary's Gate, Chesterfield, Derbyshire S41 7TD or on their website www.arthritisresearchuk.org.

STROKE

A stroke may be caused by an interruption of the blood supply to the brain or a haemorrhage. It can affect either side of the body and there may be different symptoms such as partial or complete paralysis (hemiplegia), difficulty in maintaining posture, balance or walking, incontinence, drooping mouth, dribbling, difficulty in swallowing, inability to speak normally and perhaps problems in understanding speech as well. 'Unseen' symptoms may include a change in behaviour, confusion, disorientation limited concentration, poor memory, inattention, lack of awareness of the body or disability, visual problems, impaired sensation, emotional instability and so on.

Some people may be able to accept what has happened and try to lead a normal life again (if this is possible), but others may have difficulty in adjusting to the situation and become dependent, anxious, depressed, unco-operative, resentful or aggressive.

If a person's arm or hand has become affected by a stroke, it may be possible to position it for him if he is unable to do this for himself – for example, it may be 'tight' with the shoulder drooping and the elbow, wrist and fingers flexed, or it may hang loosely down by his side. Sometimes one hand or arm may tighten up if he is doing something with the other which he finds demanding or difficult or if he is under stress, and staff will need to try to persuade him to rest or to do an activity that is easier, or to find out why he is distressed.

When someone with a stroke has to be moved, staff have to decide how to do it safely so that he does not get injured e.g. around the affected shoulder. If he wants to use a chair, it is important to check that it is stable, comfortable and supporting and has a seat that will allow him to sit well back while keeping his feet flat on the floor. He will have to try to keep a normal sitting position with his weight being taken evenly on both hips. If he is using a wheelchair, the footplates may need to be adjusted so that he can keep his knees and ankles at right angles, and any movable parts, such as armrests, legrests and so on, must be in place. A cushion may be used if he is uncomfortable, likely to develop pressure areas or if he needs to be higher in the chair.

If a table is being used, this may have to be adjusted to the right height so that he can rest his forearms on it comfortably and keep in a good sitting position.

In some centres there may be a physiotherapist available to help with positioning and walking, and an occupational therapist who can advise about aids and equipment. If an elderly person has difficulty with communication a speech and language therapist may be able to provide help.

Sitting in a chair

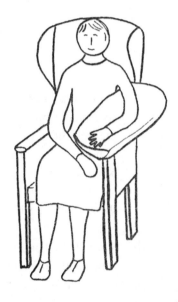

Chair giving support.
Pillow supporting the affected arm.
Person comfortable in the chair.
Chair the right height with the feet flat on the floor.

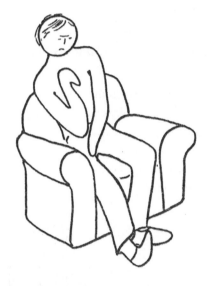

Chair not giving enough support.
Arm has become bent and 'tight'.
Person tending to fall sideways.
Foot not flat on the floor.

Being pushed in a wheelchair

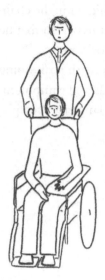

Person sitting upright in the wheelchair with the affected arm being supported on an armrest. Person is comfortable and the footrests have been adjusted to the right height.
(Note: A person needs to be assessed by an occupational therapist or physiotherapist before using an armrest.)

Attendant unaware of what is happening.
Affected hand becoming trapped in the wheel.
Armrest missing – person could fall out sideways and his cover could get caught in the wheel.
Footrest is missing and the affected leg is being dragged under the wheelchair.

A person who has had a stroke sitting at a table

Person sitting with his hips, knees and ankles at a right angle.

Chair at the right height from the floor.

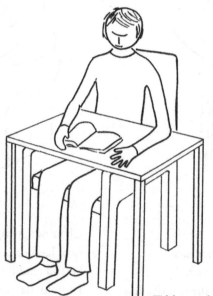

Arm and hand held comfortably on a table of the right height (a piece of non-slip material may be needed under the arm to prevent it from slipping off the table).

Hand held flat on the table with the fingers outstretched.

An adjustable table may be useful in some centres

Feet flat on the floor.

Table needs to be deep enough so that the elbow or hand do not fall off it.

NOTE: Do not try to move the arm if it is liable to be uncomfortable, painful or 'too tight'. If this is likely to happen, leave it on a pillow – ask advice from a physiotherapist if one is available.

Aids

Identity card

An identity card can be used if a person is unable to give his name and address. It is available from the Stroke Association.

Picture book

Pictures or drawings of activities or things which a person may need can be put together in a small photograph album.

Word and picture chart

This chart is useful if someone is able to point out pictures or spell words. It has a clock, alphabet, days and months and also pictures of everyday activites. It is available from the Stroke Association.

Using a table

Laptray

Wheelchair tray

Sometimes a laptray may be used if only a small space is needed. If a person has had a stroke a pillow can be placed under the affected arm to keep it in a normal position.

This may need to be adjusted by releasing and tightening the screws underneath so that it is at the right distance from the person. A wheelchair tray may be available from the firm supplying the wheelchair or a M&SRC if it has been obtained from there. (This person has not had a stroke)

Bedtable

If a person is unable to keep his affected hand and arm on top of the table he may have to keep it underneath – staff need to check that the table is not too high or pressing on the affected arm or hand. If the table has two 'legs' the back one may have to be placed behind the front legs of the chair and the feet of the elderly person so that it is nearer to him – care has to be taken to see that his feet do not become trapped under the front leg of the table.

Cantilever table

A cantilever table may be used forwards or sideways. If the 'legs' are separate it can be pushed between the legs of the chair and the feet of the elderly person. If both legs of the table are in front of the chair, it may be too far away for him to use. The arms of the chair may need to be lower if a cantilever table is used sideways.

Cantilever table

The table has to be placed so that the unaffected arm and hand are comfortable on it and the other arm and hand are not becoming trapped underneath – the knobs of the table can be used to adjust its height. If the 'legs' of the table are separate it is easier to push them under the chair and around the feet of the elderly person.

Cantilever table

A pillow may be slid gently underneath the affected arm so that the forearm and hand are resting comfortably on it in a normal position. Sometimes it may be possible to open the hand and fingers – this person has been able to keep the affected hand and arm on top of the table, (If a cantilever table is unsteady, you may have to use another table).

Single table

Communal table

This needs to be at the right height so that the table does not press on the affected arm and hand, but is easy to use. A person may be able to sit on a cushion if the table is too high or he is sitting low down in a chair.

If it is difficult to position a person at a table, it may be possible for him to sit on a cushion or use a different chair.

DEMENTIA

Dementia is a name given to the various groups of symptoms resulting from different kinds of 'diseases' in the brain.

Alzheimers disease is the most common condition, which usually occurs in people over the age of 70 though it can sometimes be found in younger people who are 'middle-aged' (this is called 'early onset dementia')

The condition passes through different stages and starts with a slight loss of memory and concentration – there can also be problems with reasoning and finding words. Later the memory continues to deteriorate and the person becomes disorientated and has difficulty in communication. Eventually the symptoms become so severe that the person is completely dependent on others for support.

Vascular dementia is associated with a restricted blood supply to the brain and occurs when someone has had a series of small strokes (though these may not have been noticed). The symptoms happen quite suddenly and the person becomes disorientated and has difficulty in thinking. There may be a slight improvement, but when he has another 'episode' the condition starts to deteriorate.

Early onset dementia occurs in younger people and can be Alzheimers disease, vascular disease or associated with another condition e.g. alcohol dependence, multiple sclerosis etc. There may be changes in the personality e.g. a person can become apathetic, restless and unaware of the needs of others – his speech, judgement and reasoning may become affected.

Many people with dementia develop various symptoms, these can include incontinence, confusion, wandering, restlessness, pacing, apathy, agitation and sometimes extreme violence and these create difficult situations for staff who are likely to need special training so that they can cope with the problems.

When someone with dementia is taken into a care he needs to feel comfortable, safe and secure and know that he is surrounded by staff who are supportive and caring. The building too should be pleasant and welcoming and with 'signs' so that he can find his way around easily – seating overlooking a garden and relaxing music can help to create a restful atmosphere.

Providing activities for people with dementia can be very difficult because sometimes they are unable to say what they like or dislike and how their condition affects them. Because of this the Activity Organiser needs a good understanding of their background so that she can choose activities which will help them and which they enjoy even though they may need to be simpler and less challenging.

(Many books have been written on Dementia and some of these are mentioned in the Appendices).

2 MOBILITY

Some elderly people have difficulty in moving about safely, and in order to overcome this they may have been issued with a walking aid. This can help to reduce pain, improve mobility, increase confidence and prevent them from falling.

Walking aids are available from several sources. They may be provided by a hospital department, a hospital or community physiotherapist or a Social Services department, or they can be purchased from shops selling aids. Some authorities loan out aids for a certain time and ask for them to be renewed periodically, or returned if no longer needed.

There is a wide variety of walking aids, including walking sticks, tripod sticks (with three feet), tetrapod sticks (with four feet), crutches for use under the arm or to support the forearm (elbow crutches) and walking frames with or without wheels. Some walking frames can be folded so that they will fit into the boot of a car, or have a seat and a bag or basket to carry objects. Aids can be either fixed or adjustable in height.

Because of the wide range available, it is important for an elderly person to have the right one to suit his particular needs. In a hospital or community setting this assessment is likely to be carried out by a physiotherapist who will also give advice on using the aid. If it has been bought privately, borrowed or obtained by some other means, the aid may not be appropriate to the needs of the person and he may not be using it correctly. For example, if it is too high he will be unable to use it effectively, and if it is too low he will be encouraged to stoop. If staff suspect this, or if a person's condition has deteriorated to such an extent that his aid is no longer suitable, it may be possible to ask for an assessment.

In a centre or home the elderly person will need to be able to use his walking aid easily and safely. The floor should be level and not slippery; carpets must be fixed and if fitted, should be level with any thresholds under doors. Furniture or other obstacles may have to be moved to allow for the normal use of a walking frame or other aids.

Rubber ferrules are usually fitted onto the ends of walking aids to prevent them from slipping. These are available in different sizes and a ferrule of the appropriate size should be fitted securely onto each end to replace the original ferrules when they begin to wear.

As walking aids are provided to suit the needs of the individual, it is advisable for everyone to use his or her own aid and to keep it nearby, ready for when it is required. Name tags or other markings will help in identification.

All equipment must be checked regularly to ensure that it is in good working order, and if staff find that an aid is damaged or worn, it should be repaired by someone trained to do this, or replaced if necessary.

If staff have a problem with a mobility aid it may be possible to contact a local Disabled Living Centre or physiotherapist for advice.

WALKING AIDS

Adjusting an adjustable walking stick

Hold the handle of the stick in one hand and support the lower end if possible. Press in the two spring buttons with the other hand and raise or lower the top end of the stick until the handle is level with the crease in the wrist of the user when he is in a standing position. Allow both buttons to come out fully through the new holes before use.

Tripod stick

Quadruped or
tetrapod stick

Adjustable walking
stick

'A' walking frame with seat – this can be folded

Delta walking aid with wheels

Rollator walking frame

Adjustable walking frame

Folding adjustable walking frame

Alpha adjustable walking frame – this can be folded

Rest stick & walking stick (the seat folds back when used as a walking stick)

Adjustable elbow crutch

Folding walking stick

Rubber ferrules

Getting Out Of A Chair And Using A Walking Frame

1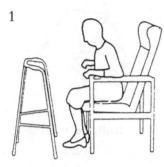

2

3

The person shuffles forward to the edge of the seat and keeping feet flat on the floor, bends forwards slightly and pushes herself upwards by pressing down on the armrests of the chair.

When standing, one hand is transferred to the walking frame, while the other hand remains on the armrest.

When the person feels secure, both hands are transferred to the walking frame.

Using A Walking Frame

1

The person places the walking frame approximately 45cm in front of herself

2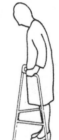

When the frame is secure (with all four feet on the ground), she steps into it.

Using A Walking Frame And Getting Into A Chair

1

The person walks up to the chair.

2

Having reached the chair, she walks round, using the frame for support, until she is in the right position to sit down in the chair.

1

With the frame securely in front of her and calves touching the front of the chair, she puts one hand on an armrest.

2

She puts the second hand on the other armrest and lowers herself gently into the chair.

3

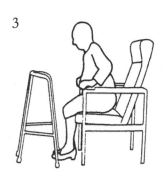

Once in the chair, she can push herself backwards using the support of the armrests.

NOTE: *Some elderly people may need assistance or supervision*

USING STAIRS

Some elderly people may be able to use stairs safely, whilst others are likely to need supervision or assistance. If a person has had a stroke or has a condition affecting one leg, making it weaker than the other, you may find that he manages best if he moves his unaffected leg first when going upstairs and the disabled leg first when going downstairs. For those people who have difficulty in using stairs it may be necessary to consider installing a stairlift or a normal lift. In a centre for elderly people stairs *must* be safe, any carpets secure and handrails firmly fixed and easy to hold. A handrail should be fitted at either side if there is sufficient room.

A person with an affected leg using the stairs

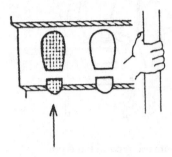

4 Moving the weak leg up.

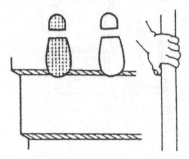

1 Starting to go downstairs.

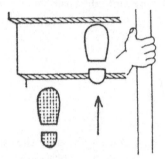

3 Moving the strong leg up.

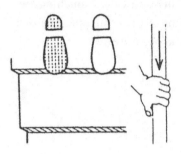

2 Moving the hand down the bannister.

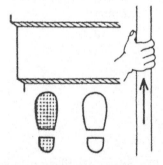

2 Moving the hand up the bannister.

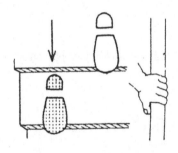

3 Moving the weak leg down.

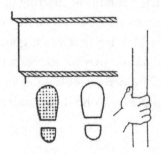

1 Starting to go upstairs.

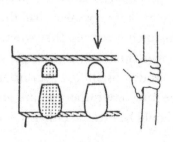

4 Moving the strong leg down.

MOBILITY WITH PEOPLE WHO HAVE SEVERE VISUAL IMPAIRMENT

by Kevin Price

You should speak as you approach a person who is visually impaired, or gently take him by the arm or shoulder and speak to him as you do so. Try not to pull or push him. When you are guiding him along, you should walk one full step in front of him and a little to the side, choosing the side that he prefers. Tell him to place his hand just above your elbow, with his forefingers between your arm and body and his thumb on the outside.

To protect both the upper arm and lower parts of his body, the person should lift one hand and arm upwards until it is level with his face, with the palm of the hand facing the direction in which he is going. The fingers are spread to give more protection. His hand should be about 20-25cm from his face.

To protect the lower part of his body, he extends his hand forwards and in front of his body, keeping the hand as low as possible and the fingers slightly bent.

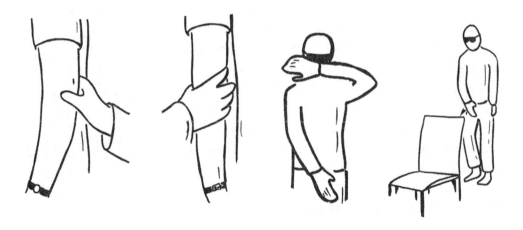

Ascending Stairs

If possible, you and the person you are guiding should approach the stairs 'squarely'. You step onto the first stair and wait, showing the person that the level has changed. You may also have to give him instructions.

You ascend the stairs together, the visually impaired person still keeping a grip on you.

He can be encouraged to use the banister if he is a little unsure.

On reaching the top of the stairs, you should take one fairly long step forwards to show that you have reached the top and that he has to take only one more step before he is level with you.

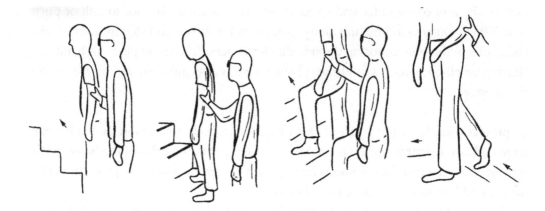

Descending Stairs

On reaching the top of the stairs, stop to show the person that the level will change. Walk down one step and encourage the person to find the edge of the top step. He should extend his arm and let you know that he is ready. The two of you descend the stairs together, the person keeping the correct grip on your arm. On reaching the bottom of the stairs, take one fairly long step forwards and wait until the other person has joined you.

Taking a person through a narrow space

In the first drawing, the person is holding on to the guide in the normal way. He is at the guide's side and one pace to the rear. The guide has moved his 'guiding' arm from the side towards the midline of his back and told the person that they are about to go through a narrow place. The person passes *behind* the guide, still keeping the normal grip, but now fully extending his arm.

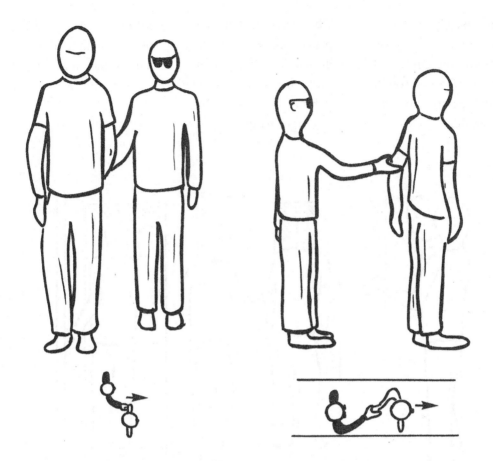

After passing through the narrow place, the guide moves his arm back to the normal position, indicating to the person that he has now passed the obstacle.

The Different Stages In Taking A Person Through A Doorway.

If possible the person should be on the same side as the door hinges – i.e. on the right side if the door is hinged on the right side. The guide tells the person which way the door opens and how it opens. He holds onto the door handle and allows the visually impaired person to pass his free hand down his arm towards the handle.

In this example, the person is holding onto the right arm of the guide (just above the elbow) with his left hand.

The visually impaired person opens the door, enabling the guide and himself to pass through – the person follows the guide.

The guide and person pass through the doorway – the person pulls the door closed behind him using his free right hand.

NOTE: An elderly person with additional handicaps may need more support.

(For more information on mobility with the visually impaired see the booklet 'How to guide people with sight problems' from the RNIB)

WHEELCHAIRS

If a person has difficulty in moving from one place to another, he may need to use a wheelchair. He may have problems with walking, a tendency to fall, limited or no use of one or both legs; or he may be weak or frail, or have, for example, a heart condition, which could be affected by the exertion of walking.

Wheelchairs are usually provided free by a Health Authority, although sometimes people prefer to buy their own (a local Health Authority may be able to advise about this). In the latter case, the cost of maintenance must be borne by the purchaser.

A wheelchair should be suitable for the person who will be using it and should have the adaptations that he needs. Wheelchairs are made in several different ways – they may be folding or rigid, manual or battery-operated, or controlled by the user or an attendant. A rigid wheelchair tends to be more stable, but a folding one is useful if it has to go into the boot of a car or be stored in a confined space. Manual wheelchairs (propelled by hand or pushed from behind) are commonly used, but a battery-operated (electric) one may be more suitable if a person is severely disabled or if the attendant is unable to push a manual wheelchair.

Wheelchairs can be adapted in several ways. The armrests can be fixed if a person is likely to dislodge them, or made removable if someone needs to transfer sideways; the legrests can be fixed or detachable and some footrests are adjustable in height. The backrest may be hinged so that it can be folded to fit into a smaller space, and it may also be extended if a person needs support for the head. Some armrests take a wheelchair tray, and on a battery-operated wheelchair the controls may be adapted and put in different positions. If a person wants to transfer sideways, the wheels on a self-propelling wheelchair may need to be smaller.

Other adaptations may sometimes be made to cope with particular difficulties – a backrest can be made to recline more, legrests can be elevated, and brake levers and handrims can be adapted so that they are easier to hold. A wheelchair may be specially designed for someone with a specific disability – for example, if he has had both legs amputated, the rear wheels will need to be farther back to prevent him from tipping over backwards.

Aids are also available which can be attached to a wheelchair:

- Clip-on ashtrays, beakers and holdalls which fit on to the armrest or backrest.
- A cushion can be added if the wheelchair user is uncomfortable, too low or liable to develop 'pressure areas'. This can be supplied by the manufacturer of the wheelchair, a Health Authority, a shop or it can be homemade. It must be appropriate for the person who will use it, similar in size to the seat of the wheelchair and of the right thickness. If a cushion is added the footrests may need to be adjusted.
- Harnesses are available for those who have a tendency to fall out, or if the wheelchair is used on a vehicle.
- Specially designed clothing can be bought for people in wheelchairs, and this is available from several companies (see the Appendices).

Wheelchairs may be available on temporary loan if they are needed for a short time – for example, a holiday, or if the immobility is not expected to last long. They could be provided by a local Social Services or Health Department, or there may be a wheelchair loan scheme in the area. There may be a charge for this service.

Parts of a wheelchair

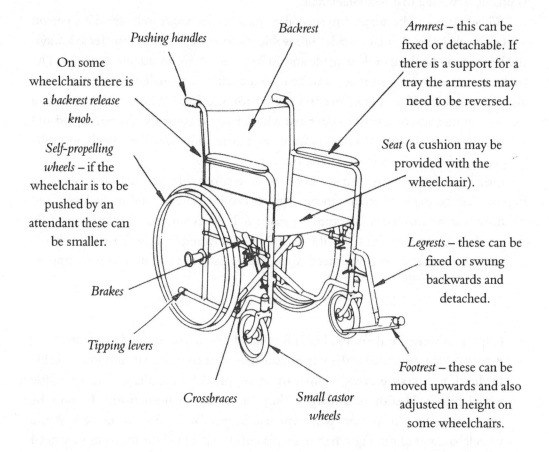

On some wheelchairs there is a *backrest release knob.*

Pushing handles

Backrest

Armrest – this can be fixed or detachable. If there is a support for a tray the armrests may need to be reversed.

Self-propelling wheels – if the wheelchair is to be pushed by an attendant these can be smaller.

Seat (a cushion may be provided with the wheelchair).

Brakes

Legrests – these can be fixed or swung backwards and detached.

Tipping levers

Crossbraces

Small castor wheels

Footrest – these can be moved upwards and also adjusted in height on some wheelchairs.

(Wheelchairs may vary – the one above was supplied by a District Health Authority.)

Adjusting a wheelchair

Adding a cushion

Fitting a wheelchair tray

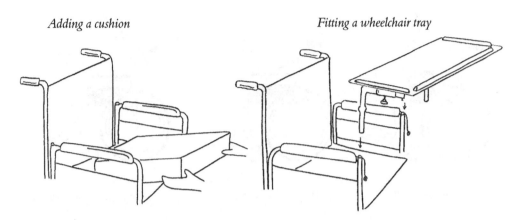

The cushion needs to be the same depth and width as the seat of the wheelchair. Suppliers usually provide cushions which will fit into their wheelchairs – these could be available in different thicknesses (if a person is incontinent the cover will need to be non-absorbant; if foam is used it must be flame-retardant).

Fit the armrests so that the tray sockets are at the front of the wheelchair. Remove the toggles and insert the tray (the screws underneath the tray may need to be loosened, the position of the tray adjusted and the screws tightened again). If a tray cannot be fitted, an attachment may be added to the armrests.

Legrests

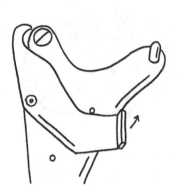

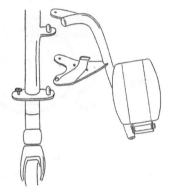

Moving the locking catch to release the legrest

Swinging the legrest to the side.

Lifting the legrest off the pivot pins to remove it (a retaining pin may have to be taken out).

Choosing a wheelchair

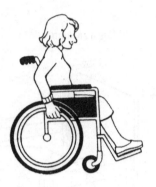

Wheelchair too small.   *Wheelchair too large.*   *Sitting in the right position.*

Propelling a wheelchair

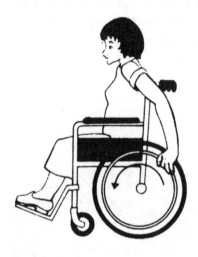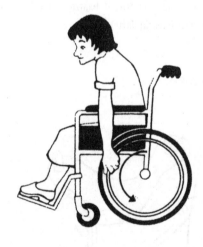

User holding the rim midway at the
back and pushing it forward to midway
at the front.

User getting into poor position as she
pushes from the top of the rim only.

USING A WHEELCHAIR

Before taking anyone out in a wheelchair it must be checked to ensure that it is safe, in good working order and not a hazard to someone else. It should be well maintained, have the necessary parts and accessories and be suitable for the user, situation and activity proposed – an electric wheelchair maybe designed for indoor or outdoor use.

The elderly user should feel safe and comfortable in the wheelchair and should be able to sit with the hips, knees and ankles at right angles and with the feet flat and secure on the footrests. If he has had a stroke, you will have to watch that his paralysed hand does not fall into the wheels or his affected foot gets dragged under the wheelchair. If there is a risk that he might fall out or is travelling in a vehicle, you will have to use a harness. Sometimes elderly people let their arms or hands drop over the edge of the armrests and you should check that these are inside the wheelchair before passing through a narrow space such as a doorway.

If an elderly person is being taken outside he should wear suitable clothing, particularly if it is likely to be cold or if he might have to sit in a draughty area. While pushing a wheelchair you should check that any clothing or rugs do not fall onto the floor or become entangled in the wheels.

The attendant must be trained to handle a wheelchair, look after the person in it and be able to cope should a problem arise. Hazards could include raised threshold strips under doorways, glass doors, steep slopes, ramps without edges, steps, kerbs, potholes, broken pavements, uneven, rough or soft ground, traffic, pedestrians and other people in the centre. If the elderly person is propelling himself he will need to learn how to handle his own wheelchair safely.

Obstacles can often be overcome by pushing down on a tipping lever and easing the wheelchair over them if they cannot be avoided, but some may be quite hazardous – for example, negotiating a flight of steps – and staff need to check that they are trained, able and fit enough to cope with this. Sometimes a mobile elderly person will be able to manage the steps safely, with assistance, or there may be a lift, ramp or subway available.

> People are advised **never** to take a person or a person in a wheelchair up and down stairs but sometimes this cannot be avoided e.g. in an emergency and then they need to know certain instructions.

At least two staff are needed to negotiate steps, and perhaps more if the person is particularly difficult or heavy. It is usually easier if the wheelchair can be taken up and down stairs with the backrest facing the top of the stairs. The helper at the back holds the gripping handles, which should be secure, and the second helper holds the *fixed* struts at the front of the wheelchair. It may be easier to remove the legrests first. The helper at the back needs to be the stronger of the two as he has to take the most strain. If other staff are helping they will need to hold those parts of the wheelchair that are not removable. In all manoeuvres like this staff must remember to bend at the hips and knees and keep their backs straight, not twisted. It helps if someone can act as leader to give instructions. If the wheelchair is electric, the battery may have to be removed beforehand to avoid spillage.

Other points to remember when pushing a wheelchair are: keep it straight if there is a camber in the road or pavement, avoid sudden jerky or fast movements and put both brakes on when the wheelchair is stationary.

A person in a wheelchair usually likes to know what is happening, and may want to discuss the details of the journey before it starts. It is also a good idea to tell him about any obstacles or manoeuvres before they happen.

It is important that each elderly person should use his own wheelchair if one has been provided for him. It may have to be marked with his name if it is likely to be used by someone else.

Points to remember

- Escalators should be avoided.
- Electric wheelchairs should only be used on a pavement except when crossing a road.
- Special clothing for people in wheelchairs available. (see Appendices)

Handling a wheelchair

To open a wheelchair, stand behind the chair and spread the armrests as far apart as possible. With the fingers turned towards the middle of the seat, press downwards with the palms on the supports holding the seat material until the seat is fully opened.

To fold a wheelchair, lift up the footplates and remove the cushion. Stand at the side of the wheelchair and grasp the seat material in the middle, at the front and back, and give a sharp tug upwards. Press the armrests together until the wheelchair is fully closed.

To fold down the backrest, slide down the two backrest release knobs on the backrest and fold down the backrest.

To straighten the backrest, put the backrest into the upright position and pull the knobs upwards (this may not be possible on some wheelchairs).

Armrests

Some wheelchairs have detachable armrests, which can be released by pulling upwards or by releasing a catch just below the armrest attachment. To replace the armrest, the front part of the armrest is inserted into the front frame socket and then the rear part of the armrest into the back frame socket. When pressed downwards, the armrest may 'click' into place. Detachable armrests may have tray sockets, which are used to hold a wheelchair tray. If this is required the armrests are removed and reversed so that the tray socket is at the front of the armrest. Detachable armrests are useful when the elderly person needs to transfer sideways.

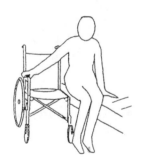

Before lifting the armrest it may be necessary to release a catch underneath

Lifting the footrest

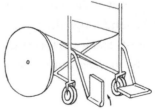

Footplates

These can be pushed to the side to allow a person to get into a wheelchair, and also upwards and downward, so that the wheelchair user can sit with his hips and knees at right angles. (If a cushion is added to the seat of the wheelchair the footplates are likely to need adjusting again.)

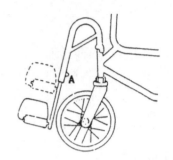

The height of the footplate can be adjusted by loosening and tightening nut 'A' with a spanner. Sometimes also the angle of the footrest can be altered by using a screw attached to the footplate.

Getting in and out of a wheelchair

A wheelchair needs to be used safely or the person in it could fall out or the wheelchair move away.

Both brakes need to be on when a person is getting in or out of a wheelchair – the brake lever may move forwards or backwards depending upon the particular wheelchair. You may have to check how the brakes work from the wheelchair manual.

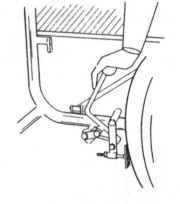

If a person is getting into a wheelchair, ensure that both brakes are on and the footplates hinged upwards so that he can reach the seat. He must *never* stand on the footplates when getting in or out of the wheelchair. (A firm object at the back of the wheelchair, such as a wall or piece of furniture, can make this activity safer.)

To get out of the wheelchair, the user should put on the brakes and hinge the footplates upwards. He holds the armrests and leans forwards slightly, and with both feet firmly on the ground, pushes himself upwards.

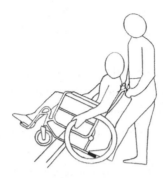

Assisting a wheelchair user up a kerb or single step

Face the kerb. Roll the wheelchair as close to the kerb as possible without actually making contact. Take care to ensure that the person's feet do not make contact with the kerb and are on the footrests. Tilt the wheelchair backwards. Gently apply downward pressure to one of the tipping levers at the rear end of the wheelchair frame with your foot and push down on the handles until the wheelchair is balanced on the rear wheels. At the same time pull back and down on the two handles. Roll the wheelchair forward gently until the front wheels are above the kerb. Lower the front wheels gently onto the kerb. Avoid jolting the wheelchair as this may cause pain to the user.

Push the wheelchair forward until the rear wheels make contact with the kerb. Continue pushing until the rear wheels of the wheelchair are safely up onto the kerb. The rear wheels should not be lifted off the ground. The front wheels or castors have no directional stability and if the whole weight of the wheelchair and occupant is put onto them you risk injuring the wheelchair user and/or yourself. This should be a pushing rather than a lifting action – this will involve using your thigh muscle:

You should be able to complete this manoeuvre without having to step forward. Throughout the manoeuvre you need to follow the guidelines on good posture including positioning your feet to give yourself a firm base of support and to make sure that you maintain the natural shape of your spine.

Assisting a wheelchair user down a kerb or single step

This is a reverse of the previous manoeuvre:
- Check the traffic
- Tell the wheelchair user that you are about to go down a kerb
- Turn the wheelchair so that the back of the wheelchair is at right angles to the kerb and step back into the road

- Allow the rear wheels to roll gently over the edge to the ground. This should not involve a lowering action, but should rather resist the movement of the wheelchair backwards
- Continue moving backwards until the castors come to the edge of the kerb
- Place one foot further back and either counterbalance the wheelchair with the other foot on a tipper bar or tilt it further back to the balance point
- Continue rolling further back until the footplates and the user's feet are clear of the kerb
- Gently lower the front of the wheelchair down to the ground (This manoeuvre is easier to carry out than to describe, but it does require practice)

(These notes were taken from the book 'Minibus Driver's Handbook' published by Hampshire County Council – every care has been taken when compiling this information, but Hampshire County Council cannot be held responsible for any omissions or errors of fact in the material amended.)

(In some areas there are 'dropped kerbs' for wheelchair users.)

Taking a wheelchair down a steep slope

- This is easier if the wheelchair can be taken down the slope backwards.
- Care needs to be taken so that this is not done too quickly.
- The occupant of the wheelchair may be able to assist by controlling the propelling wheels or by using the brakes intermittently.

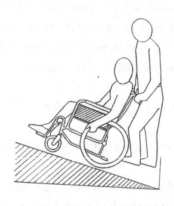

Negotiating a flight of steps

Carrying a person or a person in a wheelchair up and down stairs is a hazardous manoeuvre and should only be done in an emergency or where it cannot be avoided (it is important that it is practised before being used with a disabled person.)

Going upstairs

Turn the wheelchair until the backrest is facing the stairs, and tilt it until it is balanced. When both attendants are holding it securely, it is 'rolled' up the stairs, one step at a time. Staff may need to reposition themselves after each step. The attendant at the top is two steps above the wheelchair.

Going downstairs

With the wheelchair facing towards the stairs, it is tilted backwards until it is balanced. The attendant in front is three steps below the wheelchair. Holding the wheelchair securely, staff roll it slowly down the stairs one step at a time, repositioning themselves after each step if necessary. To avoid injury, staff need to keep their backs straight, not twisted, and to bend at the hips and knees during the manoeuvre. (It is useful to practise the procedure before using it with elderly people.) One person will need to act as 'leader', giving instructions so that all staff move simultaneously.

NB. Carrying a person or a person in a wheelchair up and down stairs should be avoided whenever possible.

Maintaining a wheelchair

Wheelchairs need to be cleaned and checked regularly so that they stay in good condition and are safe to use.

Metal parts can be wiped with a damp cloth and later dried; vinyl upholstery can be cleaned with washing-up liquid and warm water – a soft brush may be used on velour material. If a wheelchair tends to become covered with food or with mud from outside, then it is likely to need cleaning more often.

When checking a wheelchair, the following points are particularly important:

- Is the frame bent or damaged?
- Are the tyres worn, soft or cracked?
- Do the brakes work properly against them?
- Are parts of the brakes loose or missing?
- Are any spokes in the wheels faulty?
- Do the castors move freely?
- Is the upholstery worn, torn or damaged?
- Is any of the stitching undone?
- Are any of the straps frayed, worn and insecure?
- Do all the mechanisms work normally?
- Are there loose washers or screws?
- Is a pump available?

Sometimes a wheelchair may be supplied with a toolkit, which would include a tyre pressure gauge, pump, screwdriver, pliers, spanners and a puncture repair kit; usually, however, only a pump is provided.

If a wheelchair has been obtained from a District Health Authority it will need to be maintained by an approved repairer except for small repairs. If it has been bought privately, it is worth checking how the repairs should be undertaken and whether the guarantee would be affected by any work done. Often an information manual is supplied with a wheelchair; this usually describes how the wheelchair should be used and serviced. If this is not available or has gone astray, the supplier may provide another copy.

In a centre it is a good idea to have an agreement with a local firm which maintains wheelchairs, so that they can be overhauled at regular intervals and kept in good working order.

NOTE: Batteries for powered wheelchairs should be charged in a well-ventilated room away from anyone who may be smoking or from other people in the room.

Tyres

Tyres need to be firm enough so that the brakes hold and the wheelchair does not slip. Wheelchair tyres may have one of two types of valve, a 'Woods' type or a 'Schrader' type. When pumping up a tyre with a 'Woods' type valve, an additional piece must be screwed onto the connection on the pump. The recommended tyre pressure for inflatable tyres may be marked on the tyre. If the tyre pressure is lost from the 'Woods' valve, check that cap A is tight (see diagram).

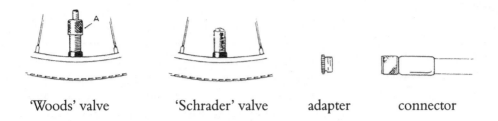

'Woods' valve   'Schrader' valve   adapter   connector

Some hazards which may happen when taking a person in a wheelchair on a vehicle lift

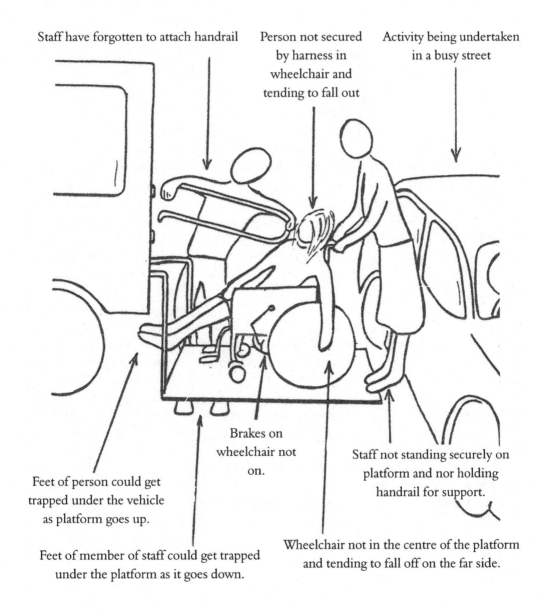

Staff have forgotten to attach handrail

Person not secured by harness in wheelchair and tending to fall out

Activity being undertaken in a busy street

Feet of person could get trapped under the vehicle as platform goes up.

Feet of member of staff could get trapped under the platform as it goes down.

Brakes on wheelchair not on.

Staff not standing securely on platform and nor holding handrail for support.

Wheelchair not in the centre of the platform and tending to fall off on the far side.

Repairing a wheelchair

Problem	Cause	Action
Brakes not working very well.	1 Brake and tyre not making proper contact. 2 Brake fittings may have become loose.	Pump up tyres to correct pressure, or check correct pressure on powered chair. (NB: Do not use air line at a local garage unless recommended by the supplier.) Reposition and tighten using a screwdriver or spanner.
Puncture.	Damage to the tyre and/or inner tube.	Replace the tyre or inner tube.
No puncture evident but soft ride and tyres need pumping up very frequently.	A valve may be leaking.	Replace the valve or inner tube (supplier or a bicycle shop may be able to help).
Wheelchair pulls to one side on a level surface.	1 Front castor on that side may require adjustment. 2 Tyres may be low on that side.	Check that the castor swings freely. If you cannot adjust it yourself, ask the supplier for help. Pump them up.
Handrims are loose and wobbly.	Probably due to general wear and tear or prolonged use.	Tighten the rims using a spanner or screwdriver.
Spokes are loose.	Probably due to general wear and tear or prolonged use.	Tighten or replace. (Bicycle shop may be able to help if necessary.)
Footrests are loose and uncomfortable.	Probably due to general wear and tear or prolonged use.	Readjust and tighten using a spanner or screwdriver. Correctly adjusted footrests contribute to comfort.

Frame bent.	Most commonly happens to manual wheelchairs when they are stored in a boot of a car and other heavy items are stored on top of them.	If the damage is slight you may be able to rectify it yourself taking care not to cause further damage. Do not hit it with a heavy object. If in doubt consult the supplier as the strength of the frame can be affected even by small dents.
Chair is stiff and difficult to manoeuvre.	Movable parts seizing up.	Oil at the points indicated by the supplier.
Battery not recharging when plugged in.	Plug and/or socket connections may have shaken loose whilst the chair is in use.	Check the plug and socket. Check fuse and reset button if there is one.
Chair does not respond to commands even after charging the battery.	1 Circuit breaker may have tripped. 2 Charger may still be plugged into chair.	Reset the circuit breaker. Disconnect the charger.

The above chart is taken from the book *Choosing a Wheelchair* published by RADAR.

3 MOVING AND HANDLING ELDERLY PEOPLE

Before an elderly person is moved staff must have some understanding of the different methods and know which one to use in each case. They will have to decide whether it can be done by one person or by more and whether any equipment may be needed.

They need to know how to hold the person's body in a good position that will prevent back injuries to themselves, other staff or the person being moved, and they must also be secure enough to control the move safely. Different moves may be done with the same elderly person at different times, depending on his ability, co-operation and condition and on the particular situation.

Before moving the elderly person he should be assessed: Is he able to help with the move? What is his condition? Is he able to take his own weight? Is he alert and co-operative? Is he heavy or large? And so on.

The kind of move has to be decided and which staff can do it. Someone needs to act as leader to give instructions if more than one member of staff is taking part in it. Everyone should be in the right position – for example, with the feet apart, back straight and untwisted, hips and knees bent and grasping each other or the elderly person securely. After the instruction 'ready, steady' and then the action word, e.g. 'move', 'stand', 'sit', 'slide', etc., staff move together, straightening their legs if necessary until the person is in another position.

If a person is able, it maybe possible for him to transfer sideways out of a wheelchair or to use an aid for support.

Many books have been written on moving and handling people. These are worth reading, but perhaps one of the best ways of learning is to attend a course run by an experienced person who is able to teach and demonstrate the different techniques and enable staff to try out the moves for themselves. It is important to practice the moves before starting to use them unsupervised.

Courses on moving and handling may be organised locally or nationally by a Health or Social Services department, a physiotherapy unit or another group, and it is wise to ask around if there is no one in the centre who is able to run one.

As equipment and procedures may change from time to time, it is important to keep up to date and be aware of any new methods which may be easier and safer to use.

(It is advisable for staff to attend a moving and handling course if this is possible)

Moving people or loads

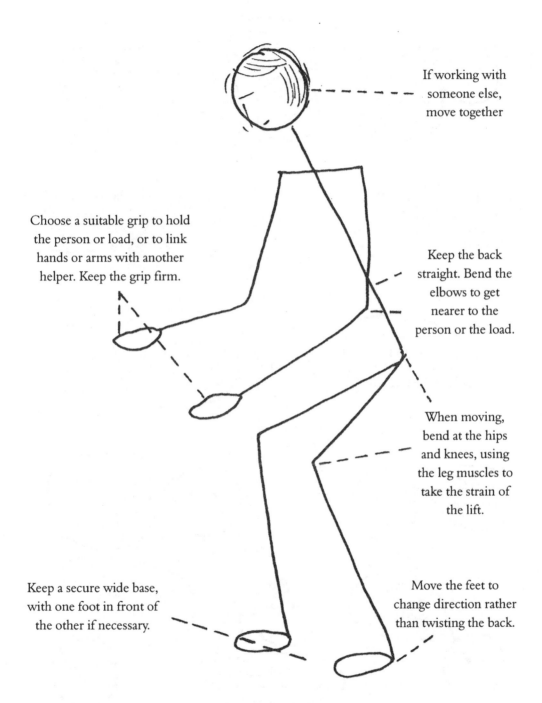

If working with someone else, move together

Choose a suitable grip to hold the person or load, or to link hands or arms with another helper. Keep the grip firm.

Keep the back straight. Bend the elbows to get nearer to the person or the load.

When moving, bend at the hips and knees, using the leg muscles to take the strain of the lift.

Keep a secure wide base, with one foot in front of the other if necessary.

Move the feet to change direction rather than twisting the back.

Some points which may need to be considered before moving an elderly person

4 OUTDOOR TRANSPORT

Many elderly people enjoy going out and are able to use normal transport, but sometimes this may not be possible and an adapted vehicle has to be used, this could be a car, taxi, minibus, coach or train.

Before going on a journey staff need to have training in the care and management of the passengers, manual handling and the use of the vehicle and equipment. They may also have to ask for 'risk assessments' on the elderly people if these have not been done. (If people are being moved or equipment used, a 'manual handling' risk assessment also has to be made.)

The person also needs to be secured inside the vehicle.

CAR

A car is perhaps one of the easiest ways for an elderly person to get around, particularly if he is not too disabled and can manage to get into the front passenger seat. (This is the best seat if someone has a mobility problem – if the car is a two door one, the doors also tend to be wider.)

The way in which a person gets in and out of a car will depend upon his condition and ability and also if anyone is available to assist him. Whichever method he uses, he needs to be safe and secure and also comfortable in the car.

Most front seats move backwards to give someone more space and sometimes cars can be adapted to make them easier to use. Many vehicles have headrests, but if these are missing, they will have to be fitted and adjusted to support the *back* of the head.

If a person has a problem with incontinence, he will need to wear protective garments and also sit on a seat which has been covered with an 'incontinence pad' or other waterproof material.

Everyone in the vehicle should wear a seatbelt – this may be a lap and diagonal belt or lap belt if someone is sitting on the back seat (see diagram). These have to be firm, secure and comfortable and also well fitting so that they do not press onto the abdomen or neck. If a person is very small or tall, it may be possible to use a 'shoulder belt height adjuster' or to add a device onto the webbing and to make a seatbelt more comfortable, there are aids such as padded sleeves, tension easers etc. Many new cars have 'inertia reel safety belts' these lock and become 'inert' if the car has to stop suddenly. (Any adjustments to a seatbelt have to follow Health and Safety regulations). If a cushion is added, it has to be secured around the back of the seat with straps.

Other aids, which may be used to get someone in and out of a car can include a transfer board, revolving disc for the feet (if he is able to stand) and a hoist etc.

Elderly people often need supervision and assistance when using a car – if you would like to know more about 'assisted transfers' see appendices.

Using a straight transfer board

If someone is unable to get from a wheelchair and into a car, he may be able to use a transfer board (see diagram). This is placed well over the wheelchair and car seat so that he can transfer sideways into the car. The boards are made of wood or other material and can be bought in different lengths and widths. It is quite a difficult manoeuvre and an elderly person is likely to need help while doing it.

The wheelchair is positioned alongside the car and as close as possible to the car seat, with the brakes on and the right armrest and legrest removed. The seat of the wheelchair has to be level with the seat of the car.

The transfer board is slipped at least halfway under the elderly person and well over the car seat. He moves along the board putting his legs into the car first and then sitting down or sitting in the car and then bringing his legs in afterwards. The board is removed.

When getting out, the wheelchair is placed in the same way and the board put underneath the person and well over the seat of the wheelchair. He slides along the board bringing his legs out first or last whichever is easier for him. The board is taken away.

Getting into a car

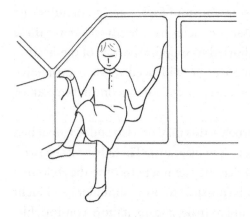

Sitting down, bringing in the right leg and then the left leg.

Putting in the right leg, sitting down and then bringing in the left leg.

Getting out of a car

Bringing the left leg out of the car and then the right leg before standing up.

Bringing the left leg out of the car and standing up before moving the right leg.

(Note: Staff need to check that a person's head is lower than the door sill before getting in and out of a car)

Using a wheelchair

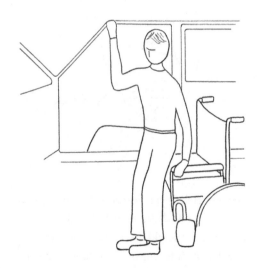

The person stands up or slides across onto the car seat from the wheelchair. He may need to use the right armrest for support or take it out – the right footrest may also have to be removed.

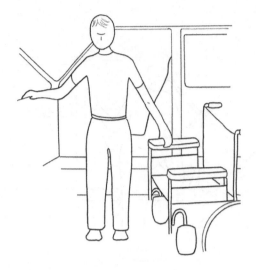

To get out of a car, the person may stand or slide across onto the wheelchair after the right armrest has been removed. If he moves over the propelling wheel, it has to be below the seat of the wheelchair.

If a wheelchair is being used to transfer sideways in and out of a car, it needs to be as close as possible to the car with the brakes on and the right armrest and footrest removed. The person has to take care when crossing the 'gap'.

Getting onto the front passenger seat of a car

Using a straight transfer board

Using a 'banana' shaped board

The wheelchair is positioned alongside the car and the board is placed securely over the seat of the wheelchair and underneath the elderly person. If someone is using a straight transfer board onto a wheelchair next to the car, the propelling wheel needs to be below the seat of the wheelchair. ⋆1 (see p. 52)

The wheelchair can positioned at an angle to the car seat and the board placed securely underneath the elderly person and over the wheelchair. (He can support the board with his hand as he moves across). ⋆2 (see p. 52)

This can be a difficult manoeuvre and you need to check that the board is secure and level on *both* seats and that the wheelchair is stable on ground which is flat and firm and is next to the car with both brakes on. The person has to be able to sit and move along the board safely – *if there is any risk to him at all another method of transferring has to be used.*

(See 'The Guide to the Handling of People' (current edition) published by Backcare).

Seatbelts

Using a lap belt (2 point belt)

A lapbelt on its own does not give enough support to an elderly or disabled person.

Seatbelts need to be kept clean and untwisted

The headrest is placed so that it is at the back of the person's head

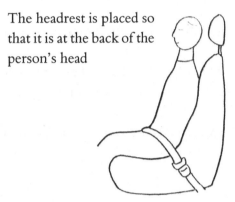

A lap belt may be fitted on the back seat of a car

The lap belt should pass over the pelvis and not the abdomen

Using a lap and diagonal belt (3 point belt)

In some cars there are 'shoulder belt height adjusters' so that the belt can be fitted to suit the height of the person

The diagonal part of the belt needs to be midway over the shoulder so that it it does not cross the neck

The 'tongue plate' needs to fit securely into the buckle

Lap and diagonal belts are safer to use than lap belts because they support the whole body.

(Note: Any equipment carried in the vehicle must be secured)

*1 The wheelchair has to be secure while this manoeuvre is being done and over ground, which is level and firm.

*2 (A curved board is used in a similar way except that the wheelchair can be put in different positions)

Taxi

A taxi can be a convenient form of transport for some people, but it is expensive. In some areas special schemes are available to help disabled people with fares.

Saloon cars are often used by taxi firms and some of these may take a folded wheelchair in the boot, though a disabled person has to be able to transfer out of his wheelchair and get in and out of the taxi.

A 'Fairway Driver' cab has an extra step and also a swivel seat to enable someone to use the taxi more easily, and in some places 'Metrocare' vehicles (from Metrocab) are used. These have space for a person to travel in a wheelchair or to sit on a swivel front passenger seat. They also allow for other people to transfer out of their wheelchairs and onto the seats. Two single ramps or a one-piece ramp can be used to get the wheelchair inside the taxi and steps are also available. On the 'London Taxi International' vehicles, a restraining strap is used to support the wheelchair and there is a folding ramp.

As services do vary from one place to another, it may be worthwhile to contact the local Taxi Licensing Office for information about taxis and schemes in the area – a 'Traintaxi Guide' has details about different taxi ranks at train, tram, metro and underground stations throughout the country. (see appendices).

Minibus

A minibus can carry a driver and nine to sixteen passengers in seats or up to five or six people in wheelchairs. It may have a side door with a ramp or lift-out step and a back door with a ramp, passenger lift or lowering suspension. The seats can be fitted into tracking, which also secures the wheelchairs.

The vehicle has to be well built and have a strong frame to support the anchorages, which hold the wheelchair tie-down and occupant restraint systems (WTORS). This can be expensive and you may need to consider sharing the minibus with other centres.

If a minibus is being bought or hired, it has to be suitable for the people who are going to use it, have access for any wheelchairs (if necessary) and also the correct restraints – the seats too have to face towards the front of the vehicle.

Staff need training on the use of the minibus and how to assist elderly people to board the vehicle and restrain them safely. *It is recommended that a member of staff attends a MIDAS (Minibus Driver Awareness Scheme) course and a PATS (Passenger Assistant Training Programme) run by the Community Transport Association (CTA).* These courses cover many aspects on the use of a minibus including driving, passenger safety, WTORS, and the use of equipment. It is important that staff are made aware of the different issues, and also the problems which may be encountered if a minibus is not being used properly. (For more information see appendices)

Anyone wanting to drive a minibus has to be capable and responsible, over 21 years of age with two years driving experience and have a full driving licence with no endorsements. He made also need to have other permits before he can drive the vehicle).

He has to be able to operate the controls and use any equipment e.g. WTORS and know what to do if there is an emergency or the minibus breaks down. He also has to be aware of the needs of the passengers and follow any policies or procedures. Other staff too need to know what to do and use any equipment.

It is important that the wheelchair tie-down and occupant restraint systems are suitable for the people who are going to use them. If a person is travelling in a wheelchair, the restraint holding it to the floor of the vehicle is *separate* from the seatbelt holding him in the wheelchair.

Getting a wheelchair in and out of a vehicle

Using a ramp   Operating a passenger lift

 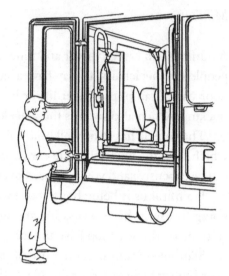

(Note: At least 3 metres has to be left at the back of the minibus to allow for the movement of the wheelchairs)

Note: Before taking a wheelchair user or anyone onto a vehicle, it is important to find out how this can be done safely. The Medicines and Healthcare Regulatory Agency have publications on the safe transportation of disabled people – these are available through their website (www.mhra.gov.uk)

If it is likely that he may fall over, an additional postural harness may have to be used to keep him upright. Other passengers in the vehicle will also have to wear a seatbelt.

Sometimes a ramp is used with a minibus, this may be in one piece or folded or there may be two separate channels, which are attached to the back of the vehicle. These have to be wide enough to prevent the wheels of the wheelchair from becoming caught in them.

On some vehicles there is a passenger lift, this is usually more expensive than a ramp but can be easier to use. It may be fitted underneath or inside the minibus. A passenger lift has to be used safely and staff need to follow the manufacturers instructions, which should be on the back of the minibus. (If these have gone missing, the supplier may provide another copy). (See page 41).

To reduce the risk of fire in a minibus, staff need to check that none of the passengers are smoking and that batteries in electric wheelchairs are secure. When buying a minibus, it is useful to check that the engine and battery have cut-out switches, that the upholstery is flame-retardant and that at least two fire extinguishers are in places where the driver and staff can reach them easily.

Gangways have to be kept clear and it may be possible to secure folded wheelchairs onto the side of the wall of the vehicle – no smoking signs have to be displayed, as it is no longer permitted inside minibuses.

The Community Transport Association will give advice on the purchase of a minibus and they also have leaflets, publications and information on how to operate legally.

Bus or coach

Bus stations may be owned by a bus or coach company, a local authority or a private company and access can seem to vary from place to place. Some stations are new and have good facilities for disabled people, while others may be very limited. It is worthwhile checking with the bus station beforehand what is available and also if there are any limitations at the roadside stops and other stations, which may be visited on the way.

The vehicles too have to be accessible and in some areas there are adapted buses and coaches which have lowered floors and fold-down ramps for wheelchair users. This facility is often shown on the vehicle and there could be special timetables for these services. (In London buses are now wheelchair accessible.)

Many companies do offer help for disabled travellers, though they may need to be notified in advance. Concessionary fares can often be obtained for elderly and disabled people in some areas and a discount coachcard is offered to passengers over 50 on some National Express services.

A book giving information about bus and coach travel for the disabled is available (see appendices).

Train

If you are taking a group of disabled people away by train, you will need to telephone the staff on the National Rail Enquiries number in advance who will call the relevant train company involved in the start of your journey. They will make all the arrangements, contact other train companies (if necessary) and send the tickets onto you.

To do this they will need to know the dates and times of the outward and return journeys, the number and disabilities of the elderly people, if they need any assistance and how you will reach and leave each station.

Staff may be asked to help you through the stations and onto the trains, but they cannot lift, transfer or carry anyone.

On many of the larger stations, there are facilities for people in wheelchairs and it may be worthwhile to consider travelling between these stations rather than using smaller local ones where the staff and amenities may not be available.

Sometimes the toilets for the disabled on a station have to be kept locked and you may have to ask for a key or get a 'National Key Scheme' key from RADAR or a local authority (RADAR also have a book which gives details about disabled toilets throughout the country)

If there is a toilet, buffet or waiting area, which is going to be used, you may need to check that there is level access and also a lift to take everyone from one platform to another.

Many new trains now have wide-opening doors, low floors, grabrails and access for people in wheelchairs though the toilets may not always be suitable. It is worth checking if these trains are running on the routes you will be using and at the times that you will need them. (Older trains may not have accessible toilets)

If someone is disabled he may be able to use a 'Disabled Persons Railcard' – this allows him a discount of third off the price of the ticket and a third off the fare of an adult companion travelling with him – the railcards are renewable after one year (or three years if a larger sum is paid). Senior railcards can be bought for anyone over 60.

Information about rail travel can be found in the booklet 'Rail travel made easy' available from rail stations, and the website www.nationalrail.co.uk/stations-destinations/ – the user types in the name of the station and then clicks onto the 'Stations Made Easy' link. There is an option of 'Station Overview' 'Accessibility Information' or 'Plan a route' – a booklet giving more details 'Stations Made Easy' is also available.

A 'Traintaxi Guide' has been produced for anyone who would like to know more about taxis at train, tram, metro and underground stations (see appendices)
(Note: If a journey is cancelled, staff on the National Rail Enquires number have to be notified)

Plane

If elderly people are being taken away by air, special arrangements may need to be made so that everything goes smoothly. Transport has to be booked to go to and from the airport and staff there have to know in advance if anyone needs care or attention.

The staff from the centre may have to check the facilities at the airport and on the plane and also at any other airports which are to be visited. Certain procedures and precautions may have to be followed so that everyone can be taken safely through the airport and onto the plane.

Access guides can be obtained at some British airports and they may also have information about travel abroad. RADAR have details about air travel and facilities which are offered by the different airlines.

Points which may need to be considered before taking elderly people on a plane

Before planning the journey

Elderly	Is everyone medically fit enough to travel by air? Do they like flying?	A form may have to be filled in giving details about your needs. Some airlines may also ask for a medical form to be signed by a Doctor. (These are available from travel agents and tour operators)
Wheelchairs	Airports may have different arrangements on how wheelchairs may be used there.	Check if you have any wheelchairs (or other equipment) which may need to be specially packed to go on a plane.
Special diets	These have to be ordered from the airline at least 24 hours before the journey.	It may be necessary to mention this when booking.
Access at the airport	Toilets, refreshment areas and other facilities.	Are these accessible for wheelchair users and others?
Services	Is assistance available to collect baggage and take the elderly people through the airport and onto the plane (on the outward and return journeys)?	If special assistance is needed, this may have to be mentioned on the booking form.

On the plane	Are suitable seats available?	A person may need extra leg room, easy access to the toilet or sit in a non-smoking area. (This has to be mentioned on the booking form)
	Is the toilet accessible for elderly and disabled people?	Some aircraft have special toilets and 'aisle wheelchairs' but staff from the centre have to assist anyone in the toilet.
Visiting Airports	Toilets, refreshment areas and other facilities.	Are these accessible and can they be used by people in wheelchairs and others?
Services	Are there facilities and help available (both on the outward and return journeys)?	Information about this may be available at the original airport.

Before the journey

Tour operator		If you have made a booking through a travel agent or tour operator check that they have mentioned all your needs to the airline.
Airport	Special arrangements	Contact the airport (about 3 days before the journey) to ask if these arrangements have been made.

On the day

	You may need to arrive earlier than the other passengers.	

During the journey

Wheelchairs		*Before* the plane leaves ask the cabin crew if all the wheelchairs (and other equipment) are on board.
Medication		Staff (or the elderly) will have to keep any medication with them which is needed on the journey or soon afterwards.
Visiting airport	During the journey you may feel that you need to ask the senior steward if the pilot could radio ahead if you have any special needs at the visiting airport.	Ensure that the wheelchairs are left at the cabin door.

After the journey

	There may be a problem with pacemakers at some foreign check-out points.	Check the instructions with the pacemaker or ask your Doctor. Mention this to the Security staff at the foreign airport.

(Note: Folding wheelchairs and some other aids are carried free-of-charge and are not included in the passenger's baggage allowance)

(For more information about air travel, see Appendices)

Many elderly people need supervision or assistance when they are moving from one place to another and **it is important for staff to attend a course on manual handling so that they know how to do this safely and also handle equipment** – a local physiotherapist may have details about courses in the area.

5 COMMUNICATION

COMMUNICATION PROBLEMS IN ELDERLY PEOPLE
by Isobel O'Leary

There are various reasons why elderly people may have difficulty with communication. Some of the conditions which affect their ability are quite common, including deafness, blindness, and general lack of stimulation. However, there are also certain medical conditions that impair communication, such as Parkinson's disease and, perhaps most importantly, strokes.

The distinction between 'speech' and 'communication' is important. The latter includes speech, but also takes in facial expressions, hand movements, reading and writing, as well as the ability to understand other people's communication.

In Parkinson's disease, motor neurone disease and multiple sclerosis, the main communication problem is with speaking, since these diseases cause difficulty in the physical production of sounds and words, due to weakness or lack of co-ordination of the speech muscles. This problem is called *dysarthria*, and results in speech that may sound slurred, very quiet, monotonous or jerky.

Communication Problems After A Stroke

A stroke causes some damage to the brain. If this occurs in the part of the brain that controls the ability to deal with language, the person will probably suffer from a condition called *dysphasia*. The language area for most people is in the left side of the brain, so dysphasia often occurs with a right hemiplegia, since the left side of the brain affects the right side of the body. Many dysphasic people have difficulties in understanding (receptive dysphasia) and in formulating language (expressive dysphasia) whether it is spoken or written. Each person's communication problems are different and what helps one person may not help another.

People with receptive dysphasia

Elderly people with this problem may have difficulty in understanding other people's speech or written material. They often appear to be understanding more than they actually can. This is because it is a distressing condition to suffer and the person may try to cover up his disability, but he may also get clues to what you are saying from your facial expression, hand movements, tone of voice or the context of the conversation; in addition, although he may only understand a few words, he may be able to follow the gist of the conversation without being able to grasp specific instructions.

Even when people have receptive difficulties, do not talk down to them or raise your voice. If their hearing and intellect are intact this approach will only increase their frustration. However, do try to simplify what you are saying, slow down and so not be afraid to repeat things. Make sure that the person has understood you. Many people will find that noise, tiredness or upset will affect their concentration and their ability to understand.

People with expressive dysphasia

With this problem people have difficulty in using spoken or written language and nearly always suffer from feelings of frustration. Often a person will know what he wants to say, but is unable to find the words. He may also make mistakes in his use of language – for example, he may say 'soap' when he means 'towel', he may produce jargon or meaningless words such 'histar', or he may make incorrect sounds within words, such as 'ken' when he means 'pen'. He may also use the words 'yes' and 'no' inappropriately. He may use words and phrases repetitively, as if he is unable to break away from the word he keeps saying, such as a swear word, or he may produce a flow of meaningless speech which he does not try to stop – this usually means that he is unaware that it does not make sense.

Do not make such a person feel rushed. He often needs time to grasp what you are saying and to formulate what he wants to say in reply. It may be helpful if you communicate with him by gesture. Encourage a person when he is making an effort to talk. Make him feel confident so that he will try to communicate, for he probably feels embarrassed by his speech difficulty.

People with dyspraxia

Following a stroke a person may suffer from an additional problem called *dyspraxia*. This is an inability to produce voluntary muscle movements, despite adequate muscle function. For example, a person may smile at you in greeting, but be unable to smile when specifically asked to do so. He may have difficulty in making movements in the right order, and this is often worst when he is trying to start the movement; once he has got going, the movement may be reasonable. Dyspraxia can affect the limbs as well as the speech muscles, so that eating or dressing may be uncoordinated. Even when there is actual muscle weakness, as often happens after a stroke, it is not enough to explain the mistakes that happen.

Typically, a person with dyspraxia has slow and laboured speech, but some words may pop out easily, such as 'I'm all right' or 'Hello'. He may be aware of errors and may become frustrated at the lack of voluntary control over the articulatory muscles. He may make frequent repeats and attempts at self-correction.

All the conditions outlined above have different effects on a person's speech and general communication. Sometimes the cause of the problem is not clear – for example, it may be difficult to decide whether a person's failure to speak or

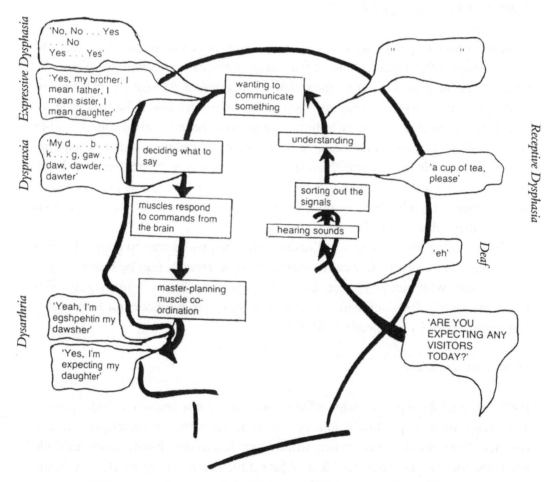

Diagrammatic view of the brain and different speech problems

communicate in any way is due to the effects of the stroke, or whether it is because he is depressed and withdrawn, or both. Slurred dysarthric speech occurs with several diseases, as I have mentioned, and can also occur after a stroke. When an elderly person uses a lot of apparently meaningless speech, staff need to establish whether it is due to confusion, dementia or the specific language problem of dysphasia. A speech and language therapist will be able to give advice on the most helpful approach for each particular person.

Definitions of words you may hear

Dysphasia: difficulty in understanding, and/or using language.
Dysarthria: difficulty with the physical production of sounds and words due to muscle weakness or lack of co-ordination.
Dyspraxia: inability to produce voluntary muscle movements despite adequate muscle function.
Dysphagia: (not to be confused with *dysphasia*) difficulty in swallowing.

HEARING AIDS

Hearing loss may be slight or severe and its cause can be divided into two main categories:

1 *Conductive hearing loss.* When the outer or middle ear has been affected, this type of hearing loss is often treatable.
2 *Sensori-neural loss.* This is caused when the nerves within the inner ear have been affected. It is an untreatable condition and is the most common cause of hearing loss in elderly people. As a result, many elderly people with hearing impairment are fitted with a hearing aid.

Types of hearing aid

Most hearing aids are now digital and made in three forms: – 'in the ear' 'over the ear' and 'behind the ear' – they may be 'automatic' where the program adjusts itself to the environment (speech without noise; speech with noise or music) or 'programmable' where the user has to adjust the aid by pressing a button e.g. to tune into a 'loop' system.

1) *'In the ear' hearing aids*

   These aids fit inside the ear and need to be cleaned each day with the small brush (supplied with the aid) and a soft cloth – the wax filter can be cleaned every 4-6 weeks. The aid may be placed in the 'drying box' to reduce moisture.

2) *'Over the ear' hearing aids*

   These are discreet aids, which are fitted over the top of the ear. They have a piece of tubing, which is attached to the earmould. If the aid becomes 'dead' it is likely that this tubing has become blocked and it will need to be cleaned with the thin wire cleaning tool (provided with the aid). If the 'filter' has become blocked, this can be changed (this is normally done every 4 weeks). The 'dome' on the aid can be cleaned with a tissue.

3) *'Behind the ear' hearing aids*

   These are worn behind the ear and are connected to the earmould with a piece of plastic tubing. To fit the aid, place the earmould into the ear first, then hook the aid over the top of the ear, placing it behind. If glasses are worn, put these on first with the aid outside, between the glasses and the ear.

Maintenance

Occasionally the hearing aid may develop a slight fault. The table below lists some common faults and solutions.

HEARING AID FAULT FINDING TABLE

Problem	*Check*	*Fault*	*Solution*
Aid dead	Tubing	Condensation in tube	Remove earmould and blow out
	Earmould	Earmould blocked with wax	Remove earmould and clean
	Battery	Battery flat, wrong way round	Examine, test and replace
	Wax filter	Wax filter needs changing	Change wax filter

Problem	Check	Fault	Solution
Buzzing noise	On/off switch	Switch on 'T'	Reset switch to 'M'
		Microphone broken	Return for repair
	Ear canal	Wax in the ear canal – poorly fitting hearing aid	Return aid
Crackling intermittent problems	Battery contacts switch volume control	Faulty connections	Return hearing aid to Hearing Aid Services for repair
Whistling	Earmould	a) Poorly fitting	Check earmould fit
		b) Incorrect mould insertion	Return to Hearing Aid Service for replacement tube or earmould.
	Tubing	Hole in tubing	
	Ear canal	Wax in the ear canal – poorly fitting hearing aid	Return aid
	Ear canal	Wax	Refer to GP

Note: On a hearing aid the following letters may be marked:
'O' = Off
'M' = Microphone (on)
'T' = for use with a telephone, television or loop system.

Earmoulds

These are individually moulded and must be a perfect fit to avoid soreness or feedback (whistling). The earmould should be cleaned daily by removing the mould from the hearing aid and washing it in warm soapy water. *Do not use a detergent.*

How to obtain an NHS hearing aid

Anyone who wishes to try an NHS aid must be referred by their general practitioner to the local Hearing Aid Services Department for hearing assessment. Some areas may still be referring patients to the local ENT Department.

If a hearing aid is issued by the local hospital it will be maintained free of charge and replaced when necessary. If the aid has been purchased from a private supplier the user will need to see an Audiologist every 6 months so that he can be reviewed. He will also have to pay for any batteries or repairs.

Environmental aids for hearing impaired people

These devices are supplementary to using a hearing aid and are designed to assist in specific areas. Depending on the locality, these aids may be available through the NHS or Social Services. However, all these devices can be purchased from numerous retail outlets.

1 *Television Aids.* A portable personal system for listening to the television with an independent volume control.
2 *Telephone adaptors.* These can assist with:
   a) Amplification of ring tone
      – extra loud bell.
      – variability of type of ring.
   b) Amplification of voice
      – speech amplifier volume control
      – inductive coupler to be used only in conjunction with the 'T' position of a hearing aid
3 *Doorbell.* Frequently hearing impaired patients may be unaware of callers but can be helped by:
   a) Extra loud doorbell.
   b) A flashing light. The doorbell is connected to either a single light (for example, in the living room), or to all the lights in the house, with adaptation for day or night usage.

When an elderly person is first issued with a hearing aid, he or she may find the background noises very distracting, so it is recommended that the aid should be used only at home for the first few weeks. Once the user has become more confident he can try the hearing aid outside, but traffic noises can appear to be quite loud. It should be noted that it can take up to three months or more to get the full benefit from the hearing aid.

Many Social Services Departments employ social workers for the deaf, or other staff who are able to give advice about aids and equipment and can also suggest services which may be available for hearing impaired people in the area. Local hospital departments, too, may have the service of volunteers who visit hearing impaired people to give advice about hearing aids and so on. If you encounter problems with hearing aids or other equipment and need information, it may be helpful to contact the local Hearing Aid Services Department who will be happy to advise you.

Batteries

All hearing aids use a battery, which will need to be replaced at regular intervals. The length of time the battery will last depends on how powerful the hearing aid is. Supplies of batteries for NHS hearing aids can be obtained from the local Hearing Aid Services Department free of charge; however, if the aid has been purchased privately, supplies will have to be bought from a local retail outlet.

(Note: Digital hearing aids have a battery warning device so that the user can change it before it goes 'dead')

The golden rules of good communication with hearing impaired people

For those who have hearing impairment, clear speech, body language and facial expression are essential as an aid to understanding the spoken word. The following actions on your part will assist in communication:

1 Be patient.
2 Attract the person's attention before speaking.
3 Keep your face visible and ensure that it is well lit; remember not to hide your mouth with your hands.
4 Always look at the person you are speaking to.
5 Do not shout. Speak clearly and not too quickly.
6 Do not break your rhythm when speaking. Lip-reading is usually in phrases, not in words.

7   Do not keep repeating the same phrase if not initially understood – change your wording.
8   Remember to write down important information such as the date of the next appointment, or when and how medication should be taken.
9   Remember that a hearing aid amplifies background noise as well as speech.
10 Use your hands in gesture whenever practical to do so.

6 FIRST AID

When working in a centre you will need to find out about the policies and procedures if there is an emergency e.g. an elderly person may faint, fall, have a heart attack or fit or go into a diabetic coma etc.

Some centres keep records of the medical condition of the elderly people and their medication, while others may not and it is important to know what to do and when to call for an ambulance.

Ambulance staff may ask for details about the elderly person such as his name and address, the names, addresses and telephone numbers of the next-of-kin (neighbour or friend) and the doctor and any medication which he is receiving. They will also want to know his disabilities, present condition and if he has taken any tablets. (This information could perhaps be written down beforehand or a member of staff may take it with her as she accompanies him to the hospital.

Food and drink may not be given to someone who is going into hospital though a person with diabetes can have some sugar).

Staff need to be aware of the medication which a person is taking so that he has the correct amount at the right time. If he has a problem it may be that he has taken the wrong dose or forgotten to take it altogether. Relatives etc. may need to be reminded if any medication has to be replaced.

In some centres, it may be necessary for staff to attend a First Aid course, this may be arranged by the authority responsible for the centre or it may be run by the St. John Ambulance etc. This needs to cover the different kinds of situation which may happen in a centre as well as the more usual subjects studied on a First Aid course.

It is useful if a room can be set aside in the centre for 'emergencies' with a bed or couch and a blanket if possible. *A First Aid box and handbook should always be kept in a place which is readily accessible.* (The box may need to be checked regularly to keep it up-to-date).

(Note: If an incident occurs in a centre, the relatives, neighbour or friend may have to be informed).

PART TWO

ACTIVITIES

7 TRADITIONAL CRAFTS

Before giving an elderly person an activity it is necessary for staff to find out from him (or his family) what he can do and if he has any particular interests or skills. Other things which may need to be considered are his mental and physical health, any disabilities, mobility, self-care, hobbies and if he has any personal choices or preferences.

NAPA (National Association for Providers of Activities for Older People) have produced a form called 'the functional performance record' which gives details about the person and his background. This is useful for the Activities Organiser as it can help her to assist the person in making the right choices about the activities he wants to do.

If someone has a disability or condition that could be affected by taking part in an activity, the Activity Organiser has to make sure that what he has chosen is suitable e.g. it would be unwise for him to attempt a strenuous activity if he had a serious heart condition or for him to go into a situation where there are obstacles, furniture or equipment if he was liable to have fits, dizziness or bouts of unconsciousness. People with respiratory conditions too should avoid attempting activities which are dusty or could give off fumes, vapours or particles into the air, this might happen if someone was sanding a piece of wood or using certain kinds of wool.

When doing an activity, the elderly person should be in the most comfortable position for the job in hand – either sitting upright with the hips, knees and ankles at a right angle or standing at a table which has been adjusted to the right height. If he is sitting in a chair, this may need to have a backrest and arms so that it gives him more support and prevents him from falling out easily.

Any activity given to an elderly person should be safe for him to do; he should not be at risk of harming himself, anyone else or of damaging property. It is a good idea for people to have their own tools and materials and to keep these in a container for their own use. This could be a box, or a bag, which can be hung on the back of a wheelchair or locker. Each box or bag can be labelled with the owner's name, so that it does not get lost or be used by someone else.

Sometimes activities have to fit in with the running of the centre – either because the main purpose of the centre is the nursing and care of the elderly people or because there may be a limited number of staff available. It may therefore be more convenient to provide individual activities in the morning for those who can manage without a lot of help, and to organise social activities in the afternoon when more staff may be available. If any other services are provided, such as chiropody, physiotherapy or hairdressing, arrangements for activities will have to be organised around these too.

In a residential centre it may be possible to plan activities for the week if this suits the residents e.g. dominoes on a Monday afternoon, bingo on Tuesday and Thursday afternoons, a whist drive on a Wednesday afternoon and table games on a Friday afternoon. In a day centre these activities may need to be staggered if people attend on the same days each week. Other events arranged could be a service on alternate Sundays and a social on the first Tuesday of the month. There could also be special events, such as a birthday celebration, an Easter Bonnet parade, Harvest Festival, a bazaar, exhibition or sale of work and a jumble sale. All these add interest and give the elderly people something to look forward to. Projects such as fund-raising for a minibus can also give a sense of purpose.

Most activities can normally be undertaken in a day room or lounge, although some, like snooker and baking, are best done in another area. In some centres, different rooms are used for different purposes – a TV room, a reading room, a quiet room, a games room and so on – and this can be useful in a long-stay unit where residents may have to stay in the same room with the same people over a long period of time.

If there are no staff to provide activities, it may be possible to use the television and radio as a source of entertainment, and also a music centre which can be used to play records, discs and tapes chosen by the elderly people.

People should always be allowed to choose what they want to do, although sometimes it may be necessary to encourage them to join in an activity if it is felt that it could be of benefit to them. If a person's disability is affecting his ability to perform an activity, it may be possible to do it in a different way or aids could be available at a local Disabled Living Centre.

In this section the activities have been divided into traditional crafts, games and other activities. There are of course many other activities that elderly people can do, but it is hoped those included may stimulate further ideas.

ART

In a centre art can provide opportunities for interesting and creative activity for those who are unable to attempt anything more strenuous. Work can be fixed to a table with sellotape, Blu-tac or drawing board clips, or it can be pinned to a board which is placed on a non-slip surface. Pencils and brushes can be built up with padding (or Rubazote) if they are too slender to hold, or extra-large brushes can be bought.

If a person is unable to draw but enjoys painting, it may be possible to buy sketches on paper or board from the local art shop which may also supply 'art kits' containing instructions and all necessary materials. Some elderly people may find these a little difficult and may prefer to do a 'painting by numbers' picture which can be bought at a local toy shop. If you have difficulty obtaining these, a print shop may be able to photocopy drawings onto art paper, or you could trace them onto art paper or board using tracing or greaseproof paper.

In some centres there may be equipment to make drawings and painting easier – easels, water pots and paint pots that can be secured, and a good supply of art paper, sketch pads, brushes and paints for watercolour and oil painting – while in others items may need to be purchased as they are needed.

Some elderly people have a tendency to knock over paint pots or water jars and you may have to provide containers that are easier for them to use – a large, flat-bottomed ashtray is excellent for holding water and supporting brushes – or you could use a double suction aid to secure containers. A water pot is available that holds brushes and has a lid to prevent spillage of water. It can also be completely closed when not in use.

NOTE: *Cleaning brushes.* Brushes used for oil paint can be rinsed in white spirit and then washed with soap; brushes used for watercolours can be rinsed in cold water, while those used for acrylic paint can be washed with cold water and soap. If acrylic paint or oil paint has dried on a brush, it can be softened with paint solvent, cleaned as above and stored upside down in a jar.

BEADART

This is an interesting craft for elderly people who are able to do it and enjoy making designs and pictures. It can be done by someone using one hand or who may have difficulty in doing other crafts. A non-slip mat can be placed under the base to prevent it from slipping.

The bases are made by putting a beadart 'bead' onto each 'pin' on the pin base, this may be a base which holds the beads securely or it could be a 'two-part set' i.e. a pin base which holds the beads loosely and a frame. In the first method the beads are pressed firmly onto the pins, in the second method the design is made on the pin base and the frame glued. When the glue has become tacky (10 minutes), the frame is laid on the beads and left to dry (about 6 hours). The pin base can then be removed and used again.

The beads can be put onto the pins by hand or using a special tool which is inserted into each bead.

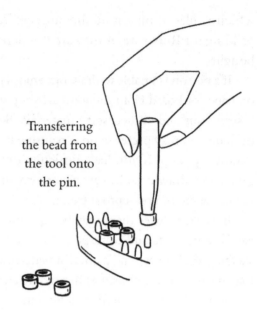

Transferring the bead from the tool onto the pin.

(Beads can be stored in containers e.g. used coffee jars so that the colours can be kept separate)

(Note: Nottingham Rehab have a selection of tubing and pencil grips, which may be fitted onto the tool if someone finds this difficult to hold)

CROCHET

Crochet is a simple and interesting craft, which can be done by elderly people while they are talking to their friends.

It is built up on a series of chain stitches, which can be used to create different patterns and designs. At first, very little is needed except a crochet hook, a pattern and some yarn (crochet cotton, nylon strip or wool, though other yarns can also be used).

Crochet hooks, can be bought in a variety of sizes and chosen to suit the yarn being used – generally the thicker the yarn, the larger the hook. Very thick crochet hooks can be used by elderly people who may have some difficulty with sight or in using finer hooks. Dark or chunky yarn is also easier to see.

Patterns can sometimes be obtained in large print, or ordinary patterns can be 'blown up' on a photocopying machine. If these are kept in a polythene sleeve, the pattern stays clean for the next person and it can also be kept in a file for later use.

Craft booklets can be bought in local shops, giving a variety of simple patterns, which can be made in quite a short time.

Method

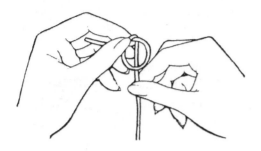

1. Hold yarn between the thumb and forefinger of left hand. Form a loop with the other hand.

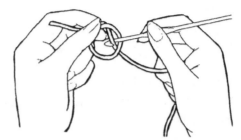

2. Draw the yarn through the loop with a crochet hook.

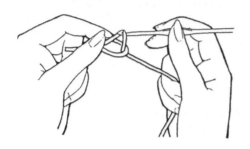

3. Keeping the hook in the loop, pull the knot together.

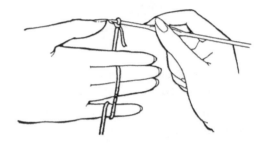

4. Pass yarn around little finger, across palm and behind forefinger of left hand. Hold the hook in right hand. Pull yarn gently so that it lies firmly around the fingers.

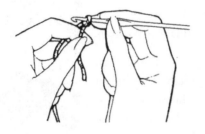

5. Hold short end of yarn between thumb and forefinger of left hand.

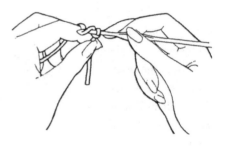

6. Pass the hook under the yarn and draw backwards through the loop.

Chain stitch

1 After making a slip knot on the hook, pass the hook under and over the yarn and bring the yarn back through the loop.

2 Using the new loop, pass the hook under and over the yarn and bring backwards.

Slip Stitch (ss)

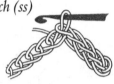

1 Pass the hook into the stitch to the left of the hook, draw the yarn backwards through the loop on the hook and onto the hook.

Half Treble (hlf tr)

1 Pass the hook under the yarn held in the left hand.

2 Insert the hook through 3rd stitch on the left, wrap the yarn over the hook. Draw yarn through the stitch and wrap yarn around the hook again.

3 Draw the yarn through all the loops on the hook leaving a new loop.

Double Crochet (dc)

1 Pass the hook into the second stitch on the left.

2 Draw the yarn through the stitch leaving two loops on the hook.

3 Pass the hook under and over the yarn and draw the yarn through both loops leaving a new loop on the hook.

Treble (tr)

1 Pass the hook under the yarn in the left hand.

2 Insert the hook into the 4th stitch on the left, pass hook under the yarn and draw backwards through stitch (3 loops on hook). Wrap yarn around the hook again.

3 Draw the yarn through 2 loops on the hook and wrap the yarn around the end of the hook again.

4 Draw the yarn through last 2 loops leaving a new loop on the hook.

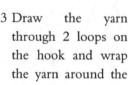

EMBROIDERY

This can be an enjoyable pastime for those who have plenty of time to spare and have full use of their fingers and hands. It can be quite easy when using simple stitches and transfered cloths or it may be more complicated.

Most materials are fairly easy to obtain, although the kits can be expensive and you may need to economise by making up your own kits and using transfers. Material with a larger weave, such as Binca, is particularly useful for those who are unable to see fine work clearly, and the *coton à broderie* cottons are easy to use with the larger bodkins. Sometimes the stranded cotton needs to be split.

If people have the use of only one hand they may welcome an embroidery frame with a clamp or on a stand, or they may prefer to stitch their work onto a standing tapestry frame. Needles can be threaded by inserting them into a firm pincushion for support and needle threaders can make the threading easier. Self-threading needles with an open end are also available (see SEWING, p. 102).

Magnifiers can be bought which hang round the neck and these are ideal for elderly people who want to see the work more clearly while keeping both hands free.

Nottingham Rehab supply scissors with an easy-cut action, and items such as pins with heads, left-handed scissors, and pin boxes with clips or suction cups are available from needlework shops.

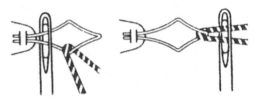

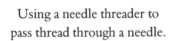
Using a needle threader to pass thread through a needle.

An aid to hold an embroidery cloth

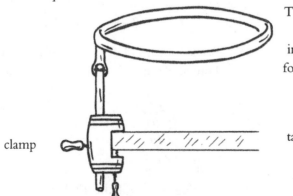

The ring can be fixed at any angle to suit the individual and is useful for a person with the use of only one hand.

clamp

table

Some embroidery stitches

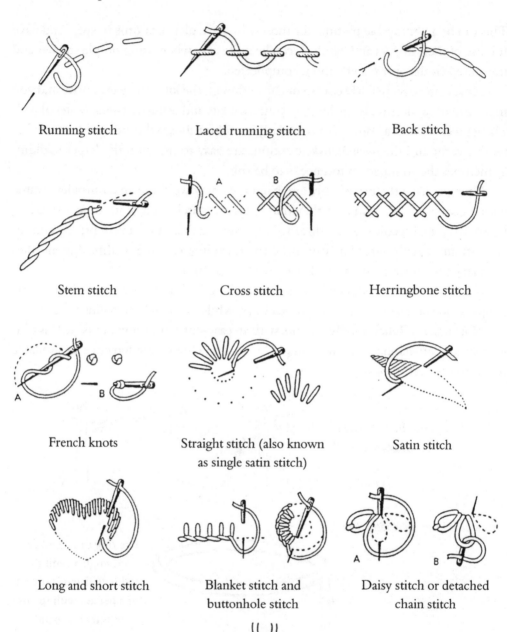

Running stitch   Laced running stitch   Back stitch

Stem stitch   Cross stitch   Herringbone stitch

French knots   Straight stitch (also known as single satin stitch)   Satin stitch

Long and short stitch   Blanket stitch and buttonhole stitch   Daisy stitch or detached chain stitch

Chain stitch

GIFT TAGS, CALENDARS AND CARDS

Items like these are usually cheap to make and are within the capabilities of many elderly people. All that is needed is a selection of used birthday or Christmas cards, some thin coloured string, a paper punch, glue for paper, ribbon, small cellophane or polythene bags, some fairly thick sheets of card for the calendars (already cut if possible), pieces of thinner card for the greetings cards (cut to size) and some small calendars.

Gift tags

These can be made from used Christmas or birthday cards or any other suitable pictures on strong enough card. The picture on the card must be appropriate – half a candle or an incomplete scene will not do. The picture can be cut out with normal scissors or pinking shears but needs to be cut cleanly and in a straight line if it is a square tag. If pinking shears are used, each cut must match the previous one. Tags can be any size, but 7 x 7cm has been found to be a good size. If the tags are to be folded down the centre they will need to be a little longer – 13 x 7cm.

When the tag has been cut, a hole is punched in the top left-hand corner with a punch and a piece of string threaded through it. If the tags are being made to raise funds, a small number can be placed in a transparent bag, sealed and sold.

Calendars

This is another useful idea which can also be used to raise funds just before Christmas. An attractive picture can be cut from a birthday or Christmas card and stuck on the upper half of a fairly thick piece of card. These are sometimes available already cut from the stationers; otherwise a large sheet will have to be cut to the right size. When cutting by hand, the desired size of the calendar (e.g. 23 x 15cm) should be ruled in pencil as a guide. If the card is very thick, a sharp craft knife and metal rule may be needed to cut it, and the card should be cut on a board to protect the table.

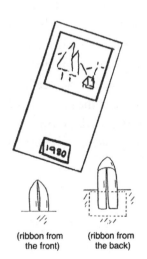

(ribbon from the front)   (ribbon from the back)

A small calendar is glued onto the lower part of the card and a piece of ribbon about 10cm long onto the top of the card at the back. A small stick-on label can be used to cover the glued ends of ribbon.

Cards

Interesting features can be cut out of pictures and glued onto folded pieces of card to make new greetings cards.

Glues

Uhu or a similar all-purpose glue can be used for sticking the ribbon. For sticking paper, elderly people will find PrittStick easy to use.

KNITTING

Many elderly people, particularly women, have done knitting before and will happily work at it while talking to friends. The scope for the craft is very wide – from simple dishcloths, pot-holders, scarves and covers for coat-hangers and so on, to quite intricate garments. Those who have been knitting for years and can still do so will be able to complete the work unaided; others may have some difficulty and may need aids to make the activity easier. Larger knitting needles, thicker wool, row counters and large print knitting patterns will all help here. If someone finds two knitting needles hard to hold, she may manage better with a circular needle. For those who only have the use of one hand there are several aids which support a knitting needle, as well as knitting frames and machines. Some people may even like to try French knitting, using a wooden bobbin: the kits can be bought from craft and toy shops.

Knitting is normally done right-handed – the stitch is worked onto the right needle – but some people may find it easier to work left-handed, working the stitch onto the left-hand needle.

One of the great advantages of knitting is that it can be continued at home by those who attend a day centre. This is particularly beneficial if they can no longer pursue their former interests, and live alone.

Stitching Seams

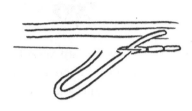  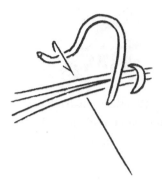

Backstitch is a secure stitch for a strong seam

Stitch which can be used to make an invisible seam

Overstitch is a useful stitch for joining ribbed knitting together.

Knitting Techniques

Casting on

Knot a loop at the end of the yarn – pass onto left-hand pin.

Pass the yarn under and over the right-hand pin.

Draw the right-hand pin backwards…

… until another loop is formed.

Slip the new loop onto the left-hand pin.

Insert the right-hand pin between the new stitches to make the next stitch.

Knit stitch

Pass the right-hand pin through the stitch on the left hand pin.

Pass the yarn over the end of the right-hand pin.

Draw the yarn towards the stitch and bring right-hand pin backwards.

Bring the right-hand pin upwards.

Slip over the other pin.

Slide the stitch off the pin.

Purl stitch

Slip the right-hand pin through the front of the next stitch.

Push the pin forwards.

Wrap the yarn around the end of the right-hand pin.

Draw the yarn downwards and bring the pin with it.

Slip the right-hand pin through the loop on the left-hand pin.

Slip the stitch off the left-hand pin.

Casting off

Knit two stitches.

Slip the first stitch over second stitch.

Knit the next stitch and pass the stitch on the right-hand pin over this stitch. Continue until casting-off is complete.

Picking up dropped stitches

Picking up 'dropped' stitches on the knit side — on the purl side.

Two ways of increasing in knitting

A

Pass the right-hand pin through the next stitch – slip the yarn over the end.

Bring the loop backwards.

Slip the loop onto the left-hand pin.

Knit the new stitch.

B

Pick up the yarn between the two stitches

Twist and slip the yarn onto the left-hand pin. Knit the new stitch.

Two ways of decreasing in knitting

A

| Push right-hand pin into next two stitches on left-hand pin. | Pass yarn over right-hand pin in normal way. | Slip the two stitches off the pin to form one stitch. | Decreasing in purl stitch. |

B

| Knit two stitches in the normal way. | Slip the first stitch over the second stitch. | Slip the first stitch off the pin. |

Basic stitches used in knitting

| Stocking stitch | Garter stitch | Ribbing |

| Knit a row, purl a row | Knit all rows | Knitting and purling used together, e.g. K1, P1, K1, P1. |

Left-handed knitting

Casting on

Make a slip knot on the right-hand pin,
put left-hand pin in the knot, bring
yarn over left-hand pin. When started
put left-hand pin between stitches.

Pull the loop made through the stitches
and put on right-hand pin.

Knit stitch

Put left-hand pin
under the stitch on
the right-hand pin.
Take yarn over left-
hand pin.

Pull the loop made
through the stitch and
slip onto left-hand
pin. Slide the bottom
part of the stitch off
the right-hand pin.

Purl stitch

Pass the left-hand pin
through the front of
the next stitch.

Wrap the yarn around
the left-hand pin and
bring the yarn and pin
backwards to form
the new stitch.

Casting off

Knit two stitches, using
the right-hand pin, slip
the first stitch over the
second stitch.

Knit the next stitch and continue
in the same way.

One handed knitting aids

Gordon knitting aid

This aid from Homecraft supplies fits easily onto the edge of a table or chair arm and can be used to hold thick or thin knitting pins.

Place the aid in a convenient position at the edge of a table and slide the clamp towards the narrow end until the aid is secure. Open the cylinder by twisting it at the top and insert the knitting pin in between the top or bottom space depending upon the thickness of the pin. (Add a rubber thimble onto the end of the pin before inserting it.) Twist the cylinder at the top until it is secure. (This aid has now been discontinued).

The knitting pin is removed at the end of each row and the other one inserted.

Home-made knitting aid

This is made from a piece of wood cut across the middle at an angle and a wooden base. The grooves can be chiselled or drilled to hold two different sizes of knitting pin, e.g. 10mm and 3mm wide.

A screw to hold the wing nut is inserted into the aid before it is glued to the base.

Suggested sizes:

Base: 13mm x 75mm x 230mm

Block: 45mm x 75mm x 50mm

Angle: 30 degrees

The aid is tightened by screwing down the wing nut. It needs to be clamped onto the edge of a table.

Curtain weights can be used to hold down the knitting,

Rubber thimble
Wrap a piece of foam around the end of the knitting pin.

Push on a rubber thimble

Holding the second knitting pin
The 'working' knitting pin has to be supported by the body while the yarn is wound around the pins. This is picked up when the stitch is being made.

88

'Easy-to-do' knitting patterns

Using nytrim:

Bag

Using 5mm-8mm knitting pins cast on 26 stitches and knit 2 rows. Increase 1 stitch at each end of the next and every alternate row until there are 44 stitches.

Knit 82 rows then decrease at each end of the next and every alternate row until there are 26 stitches. Knit 2 rows. Cast off.

Stitch up each side of the bag using a bodkin and a piece of the nytrim, fastening each end securely.

Fold each of the top edges through a bag handle and stitch down on the inside with the nytrim.

(This bag can be used as a shopping bag or for carrying items in the centre.)

Coat-hanger

Cast on 6-10 stitches using 5-7mm knitting pins. (The knitting has to cover both sides of the coat-hanger and also be overstitched). Knit enough rows to cover the length of the coat-hanger. (If using nytrim, this may stretch so that the length can be shorter.)

Cast off leaving sufficient nytrim to overstitch the edges around the coathanger, e.g. 38-45mm.

Add a ribbon or scented sachet around the hook if it is to be sold.

(These can also be made for use in the centre.)

Dishcloth

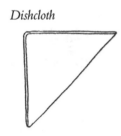

Using 2mm-7mm knitting pins, cast on enough stitches to make a dishcloth 20-25cm square. Work in plain knitting (garter stitch) until the bottom right-hand corner of the cloth can touch the top left-hand corner neatly. Cast off.

The first stitch on each row can be slipped onto the right knitting pin to make the edges even.

Crochet a loop onto one corner if necessary. (Dishcloths are one of the easiest items to make and can usually be done by most elderly people who have some ability at knitting.)

Pot-holder

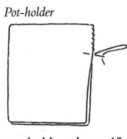

This is made in the same way as the dishcloth except that it is longer so that it can be folded over. Cast on enough stitches to make a pot-holder about 15cm wide, e.g. 25-35 stitches on 3mm-7mm knitting pins. Knit the work until it is twice as long as the width and then cast off.

A piece of wadding or thin foam slightly smaller that the pot-holder can be put in between the layers before stitching. Over-stitch the edges. Add a crocheted loop if necessary.

(These items can be trimmed and put in special wrapping for a sale of work.)

FRENCH KNITTING

The yarn is wrapped around pins or nails to give the same effect as knitting.

Using a bobbin

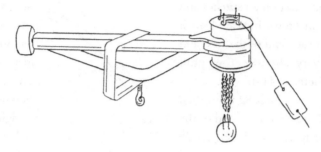

A bobbin may be held by hand or in a jar opener holder, which is clamped onto the corner of a table. The 'wheel' at the end of the holder is turned until the bobbin is secure but can be moved slightly so that the knitting can be done. When the knitting is long enough a curtain weight can be fastened onto it so that the work is held taut. A 'cleat' or weight may be threaded onto the yarn to prevent it from loosening around the pins.

Working the knitting

Using an empty wooden bobbin with four rustproof nails attached at the top or a French knitting bobbin, fasten the end of the yarn loosely over one of the nails. Wrap the yarn over the next nail from the back to the front and proceed until all the nails plus first one are covered. Using an awl or similar tool, lift the lower loop over the upper loop and nail to the back. Wrap the yarn around the second nail and repeat.

Using a frame

Using a circular knitting frame

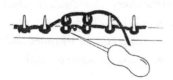

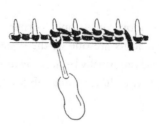

This is worked in the same way as the bobbin except that the frame can be clamped to a table or used over the knees (Romsey knitting frame). Frame knitting can be used to make scarves and other larger items.

A clamp can be used to attach the frame to the table.

Using a straight knitting frame

1. To start the knitting tie two strands of yarn to the knob at the end of the frame.

2. Pass the yarn around each peg using a 'figure-of-eight' pattern until the right width is reached.

3. At the end of the row, pass the yarn around the two end pegs in a 'figure-of-eight' pattern taking the yarn upwards towards the top peg.

4. Continue with the second row using the 'figure-of-eight' pattern in reverse.

5. When the second row has been done, fasten the yarn in a half-hitch to the knob at the end of the frame.

6. On the next row lift the bottom loop on each peg over the top loop with a hook. When this has been done, unfasten the yarn from the knob.

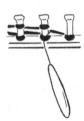

7. Continue with the knitting until it has reached the right length using the thumb to steady the yarn while lifting the loops.

8. To finish the knitting, lift off the loop from peg one and then peg two with a crochet hook. Pass the second loop through the first loop and then the third loop through the second loop until all the loops have been made into a chain.

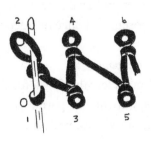

9. Put the end of the yarn through the last loop
   and pull tightly.

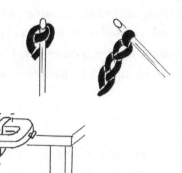

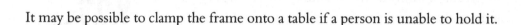

It may be possible to clamp the frame onto a table if a person is unable to hold it.

(Frames can be home-made or bought – plastic 'Classic Knit' frames from Calicoxtra are available through Amazon. To do the knitting a hook, large crochet hook and yarn needle are needed)

WORK WITH LOLLIPOP STICKS, MATCHES AND CLOTHES-PEGS

Elderly people enjoy creative activities, but they may not want anything too expensive. In this case, work with lollipop sticks, matches or clothes-pegs may be the answer. They are fairly easy and cheap to obtain, need no tools, and offer scope for quite ambitious projects by those who have a flair for model-making. This kind of activity generally appeals to men, and it can also be done by someone who has the use of only one hand.

Lollipop sticks

Many items can be made from these. Two are given here, but you can find many more ideas, with illustrated instructions, in booklets and leaflets. Both the ideas here use jigs. These are not essential, but elderly people generally find that they make the work easier and give a better result. The size of the jig will depend on the length of sticks chosen, and once decided the jigs can be made out of wood by a local handyman.

A fruitbowl
A good length of stick for this is 11.5cm and the work will be easier if the jig is mounted on a turntable, particularly for someone working with one hand. The bowl is made upside down, with the sticks being placed in alternate layers (see diagram below). It

may help to number the jigs first. In the first layer, sticks one, two, three and four are used in sequence, and in the second layer sticks five, six, seven and eight, following the slant of the jig. Apart from the first layer, each stick is glued at each side onto the sticks below by placing a small blob of Evostick woodworkers' glue on the area where the sticks have direct contact. As the sticks should lean up against the sloping blocks on the jig, the glue should be placed on the inner edge of the sticks below, a little distance from the edge. When completed the sticks should form a straight line upwards; any sticks that are warped, crooked or damaged should be discarded.

Towards the top (i.e. the bottom of the finished bowl), gradually work inwards by covering only two-thirds of the width of the stick on the previous row. When the gap between the sticks is about 10cm, make the base by first placing a set of sticks side by side on a table until the correct width is achieved to cover the gap. Two or four more sticks are then glued across the sticks in the opposite direction to hold them together. When dry, the base can be glued on to the fruitbowl.

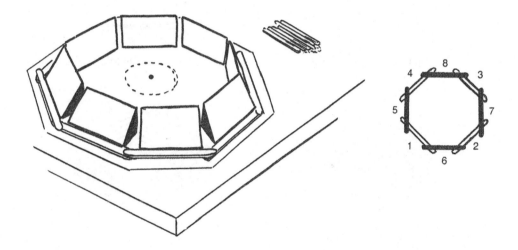

A chalet

Using sticks 14cm long, place them in the jig as shown using two sticks on each layer, a left and a right stick in one direction and a left and right stick in the other direction. Place the glue on the stick underneath where there is direct contact, using sufficient to hold the sticks together without showing on the outside. Glue each stick in sequence until you reach the top of the jig.

The roof is made in the same way, using a jig with triangular pieces of wood. The sticks are placed to slant against the jig pieces and the last stick should complete the

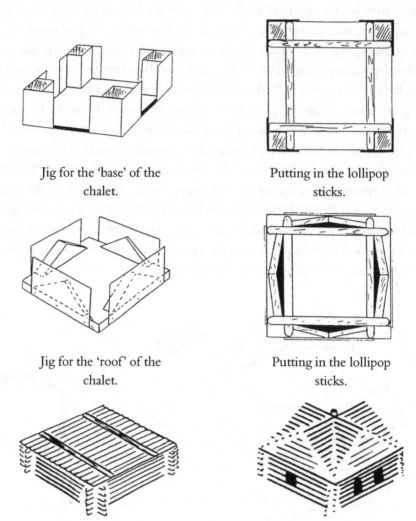

Jig for the 'base' of the chalet.

Putting in the lollipop sticks.

Jig for the 'roof' of the chalet.

Putting in the lollipop sticks.

Making the 'floor' of the chalet.

Finished chalet.

covering of the roof. When it is finished a small piece of thin doweling can be glued in the centre to form a chimney.

Form the base in the same way as for the fruitbowl and glue to the base of the chalet. To finish the chalet, glue 2.5cm mirror tiles to the sides for windows, and stick the ends of two lollipop sticks side by side to form the door. The chalet can also be sprinkled with green shunkle or artificial ferns can be added. Uhu glue is suitable for these trimmings. The inside of the base of the chalet can be lined with foam 3mm thick.

A trinket box can be made in the same way, making a flat lid rather than a sloping roof and gluing small pieces of leather to the inside to form hinges.

Match sticks

Matchstick kits can be bought, or you can use ordinary spent matches by cutting off the heads with clippers. Those who are more ambitious can attempt model buildings made out of matchsticks and it is possible to create intricate works of art.

Clothes-pegs

Spring-type clothes-pegs can be used (with the metal clip removed), and many items can be made using Evostick woodworker's glue, including furniture for dolls' houses. It is also possible to buy peg doll kits to make up.

PATCHWORK

This is an activity which can be attempted without a lot of difficulty and expense as odd pieces of material from other activities can be used. A wide range of articles can be made, from tea cosies to bedspreads, and it may be possible to get some of the elderly people to sit together as a group to do some of the larger projects. Templates of the different shapes can be purchased at a local shop or they can be made by hand from card or other strong material. Complete kits can also be bought.

Using a template, mark out the shapes onto a piece of fabric and leave about 7mm of material around each shape to turn underneath. Cut out the shape with the extra material. Mark out the same shapes onto a piece of fairly stiff paper (without the allowance), cut out and place the paper piece onto the wrong side of the fabric shape and pin if necessary. Fold the fabric gently over the paper, following one edge at a time, and tack each side when complete. Press the edges with an iron and lay the completed shapes into a pattern. Oversew the edges together, remove the paper and tacking threads and press again. Add additional material underneath the shapes or around the edges if necessary.

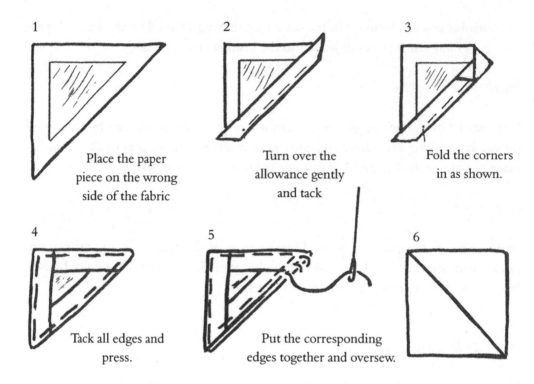

1 Place the paper piece on the wrong side of the fabric

2 Turn over the allowance gently and tack

3 Fold the corners in as shown.

4 Tack all edges and press.

5 Put the corresponding edges together and oversew.

6

POM-POM TOYS

Sometimes it may be very difficult to find an activity that an elderly person can manage to do. He may have limited mental faculties, or be so disabled that most activites are impossible or unsafe for him.

People like this may be able to make a simple pom-pom toy – two woollen balls knotted together to make the head and body of, say, an Easter chicken. These toys are easy to make, need no tools or equipment and can be done by someone in bed or with a severe visual impairment. All you will need are a few pairs of cardboard rings, several small balls of wool, some oddments of felt and glue.

To make a pom-pom toy, cut two pairs of cardboard rings, one pair slightly smaller than the other. They can be any size, but useful sizes are small rings 7cm across with a 3cm hole and larger rings 10cm across with a 4cm hole. Using 4-ply or 6-ply wool in an appropriate colour (yellow for a chicken), wind several small balls of wool which will pass through the holes in the centre of the rings. Take one pair of rings and start to wrap the wool round both pieces, showing the elderly person how it is done. When the pair of rings is fully wrapped and the centre hole is nearly full, take a pair of scissors and cut the wool between the cardboard rings. Wrap two pieces of the remaining wool around the centre of the cut wool between the cardboard pieces, pull tightly and make a secure knot, leaving a loop to hang up the pom-pom or to tie onto another ball. Remove the cardboard pieces.

When the two balls for the toy are complete, tie together securely and cut two circles of felt for the eyes and a shaped piece for the beak. If you are making an animal such as a cat or a rabbit, you will also need to cut shaped pieces for the ears. These are fitted and glued into the wool. Shaped pieces can also be glued underneath the toy for the feet. Trim with a ribbon around the neck.

A confused elderly person may be able to do no more than wrap the wool around the cardboard pieces but can get much satisfaction from seeing the completed toy.

Items needed

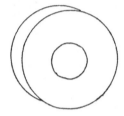

Small pair of cardboard rings
for the head.

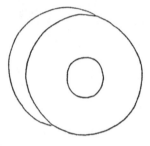

Larger pair of cardboard rings
for the body.

Glue to stick felt pieces
into the wool.

Small balls of wool.

Kits
Pom-pom toy kits are available in some toy shops.

Making a pom-pom toy

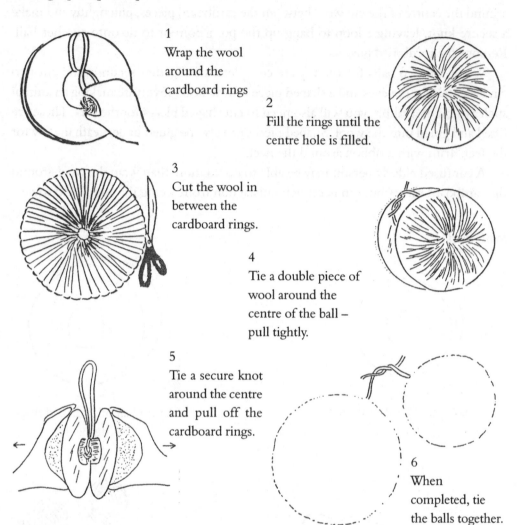

1
Wrap the wool around the cardboard rings

2
Fill the rings until the centre hole is filled.

3
Cut the wool in between the cardboard rings.

4
Tie a double piece of wool around the centre of the ball – pull tightly.

5
Tie a secure knot around the centre and pull off the cardboard rings.

6
When completed, tie the balls together.

Felt pieces for the toy – these can usually be stuck on with Uhu glue.

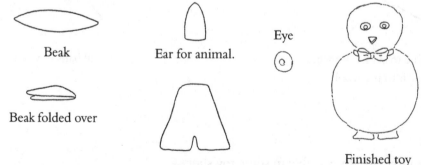

Beak

Ear for animal.

Eye

Beak folded over

Finished toy

(The ears and beak are stuck in between the wool.)

RUG-MAKING

This useful craft, popular with both men and women, can be done in several ways. Rugs can be stitched, using long lengths of rug wool and a bodkin to sew stitches such as double cross-stitch, or they can be pegged, using a rug hook with short lengths of rug wool. The canvas can be bought in different widths off a roll or it may be part of a kit, with a pattern marked on it. Even those who have a visual impairment can make rugs, but they may need a sighted person to peg the outline of the pattern before they begin.

Rug-making may be done with two hands or one-handed, by attaching the canvas to a home-made frame which can be clamped onto a table or chair arm. If two people are working on a pegged rug at the same time from opposite directions, one will need to use the one-handed method while the other works with both hands, so that the pile of the wool lies in the same direction. If they are working from the same end they must follow the same method.

Some elderly people who are frail or have a serious heart condition may find this activity a little strenuous, and someone with a chest complaint may have difficulty in working with certain types of wool.

It may be best for a person to start with a small plain rug before attempting a larger or more ambitious one, but once he has become proficient he may like to experiment with his own designs and colours.

NOTE: If the rug wool is thin, several strands may have to be worked together.

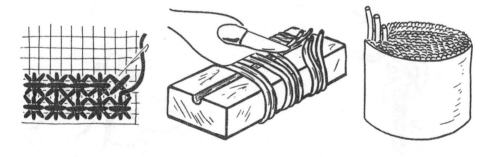

Double cross-stitch.　　Cutting rug wool on a wooden block.　　Cut rug wool.

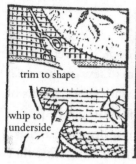
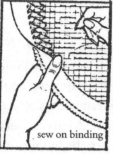

trim to shape

whip to underside

sew on binding

Starting

Finishing

Finishing off a circular or stitched rug

Starting and finishing a 'pegged' rug.

Rug-making techniques

One-handed method

1 Place a piece of folded, cut wool behind the latchet.

2 Push the hook down through one square and up through the one immediately in front.

3 Put the two ends of the wool into the 'eye' of the hook and pull the hook back through the loop, giving it a flick upwards at the same time.

4 Pull lightly on the two ends of the wool to tighten the knot.

Two-handed method

1 Push the hook under the double thread of the canvas until the latchet is through the canvas, then catch the loop of a folded piece of wool.

2 Pull the hook until the loop of the wool comes under the canvas threads.

3 Push the hook and the latchet back through the loop of wool and catch the hook around both ends of the wool held in the fingers.

4 Pull the hook back, bringing the wool ends through the loop.

4 Pull lightly on the two ends of wool to tighten the knot.

SEWING

This is a popular activity which elderly people may be able to do without too much difficulty. Some may enjoy simple hand-sewing, such as making draught-excluders, aprons and cushions, while others may prefer more intricate work.

Simple patterns (for example, McCall's easy stitch patterns) are available for anyone who would like to try dressmaking. If a person has a deformity, the pattern may need to be altered to fit.

In hand-sewing, a person with the use of only one hand may like to try using a firm foam wedge covered in vinyl. Non-slip material (Dycem) is stitched on top of the wedge to prevent the material from slipping, and also underneath to stop the wedge from slipping off the table.

To help those with a disability there are self-threading needles, pincushions which clip onto the wrist, left-handed scissors and easy-to–use scissors, pendant magnifiers which hang around the neck and magnifiers that clamp onto a table or chair arm, needle threaders, pins with large heads, and Helping Hands, special pick-up sticks with magnets for retrieving pins and so on.

Foam wedge for a one-handed sewer

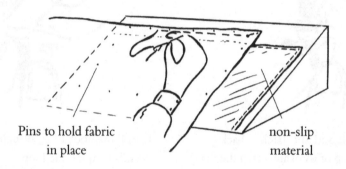

Pins to hold fabric
in place

non-slip
material

Self-threading needle

Needles may be inserted into a firm surface (e.g. cork or a pin cushion) for threading with one hand.

SOFT TOYS

Some elderly people enjoy making soft toys, particularly if they have grandchildren or other young relatives. Simple toy kits are usually easy to make, although the elderly person needs to be able to see, use a needle and thread safely and understand any instructions. Toy kits are often expensive, so if one or more people enjoy making them it may be worthwhile buying a length of fur fabric or similar material, a bag of stuffing and the eyes, felt, cottons, ribbon and joints separately. Pliers may be needed to attach the eyes and fix any joints.

When using a length of fur fabric, place it on a table face downwards so that the pattern pieces can be marked out on the back – be sure to check the direction of the pile, nap or design before doing this. Some pattern pieces are paired – that is, each body part, such as the arms and legs, has two pieces – and when cutting these out the pattern piece should be reversed the second time so that the two pieces can be sewn together in the same direction. It is wise to check that there is enough material before cutting out the pieces.

After the pieces have been cut out, add any safety eyes to the head pieces (these may have a stem and fastener or a stalk which has to be twisted and compressed with pliers); the ears can be stitched into the head pieces or added later when they have been sewn together. Ears can be strengthened with buckram or similar stiff material or lightly padded.

Follow the instructions given with the toy, using a suitable stitch such as backstitch to sew the pieces together. You will need to leave gaps in the seams so that any joints can be attached and stuffing inserted. The latter should be well compressed to make the toy firm and stable – the knob end of a knitting needle can be used for this purpose. After stitching up the gaps, other parts can be added – felt pads on the paws, stitching on the face to represent eyes, nose and mouth, and a ribbon tied round the neck. The toy may even be dressed.

If the same toys are made often, it may be helpful to make cardboard templates of the pattern pieces so that they can be used regularly. These should be marked in the same way as the pattern pieces and should show the number of the pattern and the total number of pieces required.

Any toys not bought by the elderly people themselves can be auctioned or raffled, or sold to visitors or at a sale of work to raise funds for the centre.

Some stitches used in toymaking

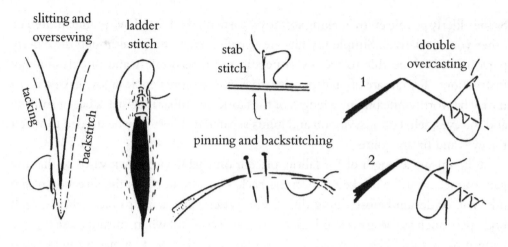

Making a soft toy

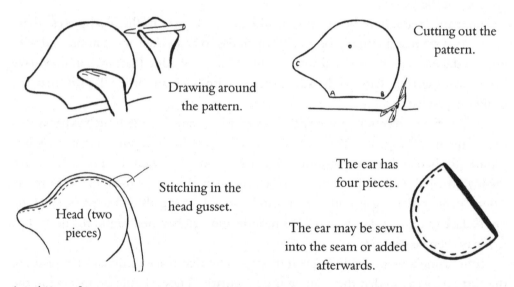

Drawing around the pattern.

Cutting out the pattern.

Head (two pieces)

Stitching in the head gusset.

The ear has four pieces.

The ear may be sewn into the seam or added afterwards.

Attaching safety eyes

After putting the stem of the eye through a hole in the material, press on the disc. This is usually done by hand, but sometimes a tool may be needed. (The teeth of the disc should face away from the eye.) When complete, check that the eye is secure.

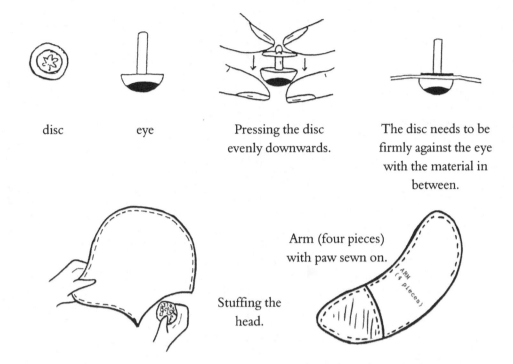

disc   eye   Pressing the disc   The disc needs to be
evenly downwards.   firmly against the eye
with the material in
between.

Arm (four pieces)
with paw sewn on.

Stuffing the
head.

BOOK-KEEPING

If you are doing craftwork in a centre you may have to keep certain records so that you can order materials, know how much you have in stock and issue receipts to people who have paid for items. This may mean having an order book, stock book or cards and a receipt book.

An order book is essential when ordering materials. This may be a simple duplicate book or it could be provided by the organisation responsible for running the centre. It needs to give the date, supplier, the goods ordered, the amount, any reference number or other details, the name of the centre, the address to where the goods are to be delivered and the signature of the person who is making out the order. Items may be paid by cheque with the order, after delivery or by the authority responsible for the centre.

When the goods arrive, they need to be written down on stock cards or in a book – staff can alter these as they use the materials and they can be checked for re-ordering.

No 81

From _____ Date

To _____

_____ _____

_____ _____

Dear Sir,

     Please supply us with the
following:-

_____

_____

_____

_____

_____

_____

_____

_____

Signed
Position

Item _____

Date	Stock in	Stock out	Stock left

Sample of an order form (this may have several copies)

Sample of a page from a stock book.

Item _____

Date	Stock in	Stock out	Stock left

A stock card

No 349

Centre _____ Date _____

Received with thanks

_____ £ _____

_____

_____

_____

Signed _____

A receipt book (this may have one or two copies).

8 GAMES

BINGO

This light-hearted game can give elderly people much fun and pleasure, particularly if there are prizes to be won.

Each person has a bingo card with 15 numbers, which he has to cover as they are called out. The first person to fill his card shouts, 'Bingo!' and wins the game. The numbers can be covered with normal counters, small squares of wood, painted ridged bottle tops, or they may be specially adapted so that people with poor hand function can hold them more easily. If someone is partially sighted, it may be possible to blow up the bingo card on a photocopying machine, or to mark out a card with larger numbers. The new card can then be stuck down on a stronger piece of card and covered with transparent Fablon to make it more hardwearing. Blind players may like to use a plastic bingo board with shutters, which can be adapted with Braille markings. These can be put on labels and stuck beside each number on the board. The braille numbers are made by using a braille frame and awl on self-adhesive labels obtainable from the RNIB. Ideally a blind person should have his own bingo board so that he can memorise the numbers beforehand.

Bingo cards can also be enlarged and laminated so that elderly people can use felt tip pens on them and the marks removed afterwards.

The caller has a bag of numbered discs, and as she calls each number she places it on a marked board. When a person shouts 'Bingo' his card can be checked against the board.

To make the game more fun, certain names can be used with some of the numbers. These include:

Kelly's eye – No.1   Two little ducks – 22
Downing Street – No. 10   Clickety-click – 66
Legs eleven – No.11   Two ladies – 88
Coming of age – 18   Top of the house – 90
Key of the door – 21   and so on.

On its own – No. 1, 2, etc.   All the twos, threes
Blind 20, 30, etc.

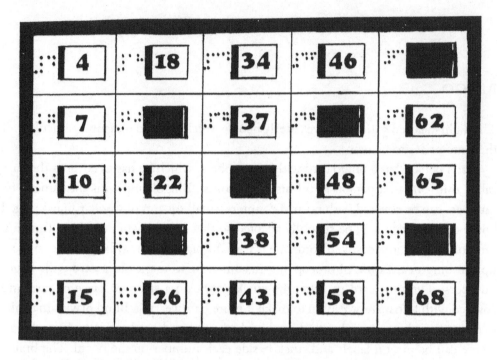

Adapted bingo board for the blind (it may be possible to get rejects from amusement arcades). Large print, wipe clean bingo cards are also available from NRS Healthcare.

Those who are deaf may find it easier to play if they can sit near the front and face the caller.

To play, the participants may pay for each game or a number of games and the money raised can be used to buy prizes. Large bags of miniature sweets such as Mars bars have been found to be popular prizes and they are inexpensive to buy. Care needs to be taken to see that the prize is suitable for the person receiving it – for example, a person with diabetes will need diabetic sweets or a different prize.

BILLIARDS AND SNOOKER

These can be popular games in a centre, particularly if there are people who enjoy watching or playing them. They are not too strenuous for elderly people and can be used in competitions either in the centre or between centres. Players with the use of only one hand may be able to rest the cue over the wrist of the affected hand, or it can be placed through the bristles of an upturned brush. An aid can also be bought to support the cue. People in wheelchairs may need a shorter cue and ask for assistance from the staff from time to time.

Billiards

This is a more intricate game than snooker and may be less popular with some elderly people who may have difficulty in remembering the various rules. The aim of the game is to score as many points as possible and to reach a certain number of points or lead after a certain length of time. Points can be scored by hitting the other two balls in the same shot or by potting a ball. This may be the cue ball which has hit another ball, or it may be the other ball itself.

Snooker

In snooker the object of the game is to pot the coloured balls into the pockets around the table. This has to be done in sequence – a red ball, then a coloured ball, and so on until all the red balls are off the table. (The coloured balls are retrieved and replaced on their 'spot.') When only the coloured balls remain, these have to be potted in order according to their number of points – yellow (two points), green (three points), brown (four points), blue (five points), pink (six points) and black (seven points). The red balls count as one point each. The person with the higher number of points wins the game.

Equipment needed for both games is quite simple – a cue for each player, chalk (to roughen the end of the cue), three balls for billiards (one red and two white), 22 balls for snooker (one white, 15 red and one of each of the six colours), a triangle to position the red balls, a scoring board and a billiards/snooker table. A full-sized table is 12 feet long, but a smaller table may be more suitable for a centre; others have folding legs, or a table top can be placed on top of a normal table (this may need to be clamped to make it secure).

Two ways of supporting a cue using one hand

 A person who has had a stroke may be able to control a cue on top of the wrist on the affected side.

 Non-slip material under a flat brush may help to prevent it from slipping.

Setting up a table for billiards or snooker

Billiards

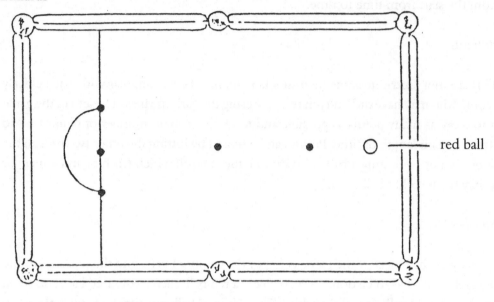

red ball

Balls: ○ White ball   } given to each of
        ⊙ White ball with spots } the players
        ○ Red ball placed on 'The Spot'

Snooker

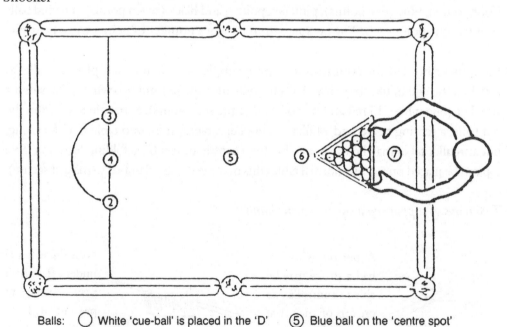

Balls: ○ White 'cue-ball' is placed in the 'D'   ⑤ Blue ball on the 'centre spot'
       ② Yellow ball   ⑥ Pink ball on the 'pyramid spot'
       ③ Green ball } these are placed on   ⑦ Black ball on 'the spot'
       ④ Brown ball } the 'baulk line'

The fifteen red balls are placed in the triangle which is then removed. The space in the 'D' is used to start the game with a white ball or if a coloured ball has been pocketed and has to be returned to the table.

INDOOR BOWLING

Indoor bowling can be played on a carpet or 'mat' in a centre or Community Hall or on a large 'rink' or mats in a Sports Hall.

It may be done in different ways depending upon the size of the room, the facilities available and also the skills of the players.

Boccia (called 'botcha')

Boccia is a game of bowling, which may be played by a person with a disability. The balls are easier to hold and can be rolled, thrown or kicked towards the 'Jack'.

It can be done on a surface which is suitable, safe, smooth, level and convenient and accessible for someone in a wheelchair. It also has to be away from anyone else who may be in the area. A wooden or tiled floor is recommended though it can be played on grass or tarmac or in a Sports Hall or room in the centre. In some places there may be a specially marked out court.

The game is played with 12 Boccia balls. These are made in sets of 2 colours (6 of one colour and 6 of another colour) and a white target ball or 'Jack'. If there are 2 players, they have 6 balls each or there can be 2 teams of 3 people using 2 balls each.

The aim of the game is to try and send a ball as near as possible towards the Jack. Any ball or balls nearest to it at the end of the game and not belonging to the opponent scores a point each. If there are 2 balls from different sides at the same distance from the Jack, no points are scored.

The National Boccia Federation has information on the game for anyone who would like to know more about it (see Appendices)

Carpet Bowling

Carpet Bowls can be played in a centre if there is enough carpet 3-6 metres long and 2 metres wide and space for any bowls which may go astray. The game has to be done safely and needs to be away from furniture and objects which could become damaged by the bowls and also from other people who could be using the centre.

It is played in the same way as Lawn Bowls. The first player throws the 'Jack' and other players take it in turn to send a bowl as near as possible to it. A point is scored for the bowl which is nearest to the Jack at the of the game and for any other bowls which are nearer to the Jack than those of the opponent. In a tie, each person or team wins a point. A bowl becomes 'dead' if it is fouled, hits another object or leaves the carpet or area.

The game can be played by 2 players with 2 pairs of bowls each or by 3 or 4 players with 1 pair of bowls each. If there are 4 players they may like to play in 2 teams.

The carpet has to be level and with a short pile, though if it is too smooth there will not be enough 'drag' on the bowls. These are smaller than normal (2" or 2½" in diameter) and have a 'bias' on the opposite side to the coloured spot. They may be easier for some people to hold.

Players need to stand in the same place while playing the game, though some elderly people may prefer to sit in a chair or wheelchair. Care has to be taken to see that they do not fall off the chair while playing the game.

OUTDOOR BOWLING

Outdoor bowling may be played on a flat 'rink' green or a crown green where the middle is higher. Flat green bowling can be played by 2 players on their own or by teams of 2, 3 or 4 people. Each player has a set of 4 bowls (except if he is in a team of more than 2 people). In crown green bowling, there are 2 players who have 2 bowls each. Bowls are specially marked so that each player can recognise his own.

A bowl may be made of wood, rubber or composition and is available in different sizes. An elderly or disabled person may choose a smaller, lighter size e.g. 00-4 and may want to try out different bowls until he finds one which is comfortable to hold. Bowls are also made with a 'bias', which makes them run in a curve. In flat green bowling, there is a limit to the size and weight of a bowl which can be used, but in crown green bowling the choice is much wider.

To start the game the 'Jack' or small ball is played and then each player in turn has to try and deliver a bowl so that it gets as near as possible to it. The person with a bowl nearest to the Jack at the end of the game wins.

Games are usually played from alternate 'ends', but if there are elderly or disabled people they may find it easier to play all their games from the same end with the staff retrieving the bowls after each game. A flat green can be divided into 'rinks' or strips so that several groups of people can play games at the same time. In crown green bowling, games are played criss-cross over the centre of the green.

Before using a Bowling Green, it may be necessary to get permission from the organisation, which is responsible for it e.g. a Local Authority, parks department, bowling club or other group. This is particularly important if you want to take disabled

Short-mat bowling

Short-mat bowling is played on a 'rink mat' 40-45 feet long and 6 feet wide, so quite a large space is needed if it is to be played in a centre.

A 'fender' or barrier is fitted at the ends of the mat to prevent the bowls from rolling off it and a 'delivery mat' is placed in between the 'delivery mat lines'. A player has to keep one foot on or above this and a second foot in between the 'delivery lines' as he plays the bowl.

In the centre of the mat is a 'block' or obstacle which the players have to try and avoid as they send their bowls towards the 'Jack' at the far end of the mat. This is placed on the 'Jack line' at the beginning of the game.

The aim is for each player to play a bowl so that it gets as near as possible to the Jack. The ball or balls nearest to it, not belonging to the opponent, at the end of the game score 1 point each.

Short-mat bowling can be played by 2 people or by 2 teams of 2, 3 or 4 players. Each person can have 2, 3 or 4 bowls each except if he is in a team of 4 when he can only have 2 bowls. These are played alternately between players or teams.

Bowls are made for the game and have a 'bias' so that they run in a curve. Bias 3 bowls are recommended for short-mat bowling.

The game can be played by someone sitting in a chair or wheelchair, though if a wheelchair is used the fender can be removed from the delivery end. Sometimes a board has to be placed over the mat so that it does not become stretched by the wheelchair.

The English Short Mat Bowling Association has information about the game and equipment can be obtained from several companies (see Appendices)

Mat used for short-mat bowling.

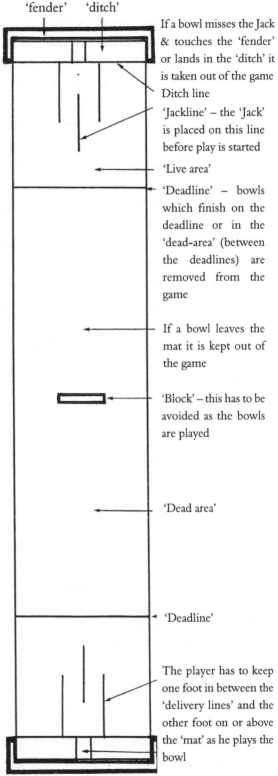

'fender' 'ditch'

If a bowl misses the Jack & touches the 'fender' or lands in the 'ditch' it is taken out of the game

Ditch line

'Jackline' – the 'Jack' is placed on this line before play is started

'Live area'

'Deadline' – bowls which finish on the deadline or in the 'dead-area' (between the deadlines) are removed from the game

If a bowl leaves the mat it is kept out of the game

'Block' – this has to be avoided as the bowls are played

'Dead area'

'Deadline'

The player has to keep one foot in between the 'delivery lines' and the other foot on or above the 'mat' as he plays the bowl people or equipment onto the green. It may also be in use for a match.

A person in a wheelchair may be able to play at bowls if it is possible to place a ramp over the edge and 'ditch' and onto the green. The wheelchair has to stay on the ramp so that it does not come into contact with the grass. The Thistle Foundation has drawings of a ramp, which can be used in bowling, and there is also a 'Bradshaw Bowls Buggy' for some who would like to move onto the green. (See Appendices).

If there are several people in wheelchairs who want to play, it may be easier if only one person plays at a time, so that the wheelchairs are not being taken on and off the ramp continually. Anyone playing alongside a wheelchair user has to be at the same distance from the Jack.

If there is someone with a visual impairment it may be possible to teach him how to play at bowls though the instructor will have to know about the different methods which can be used. (See Appendices)

An elderly person may need to wear warm clothing while on the Bowling Green and will also have to wear smooth-soled shoes without heels. A 'skip-stick' is available for anyone who has to use a walking stick while bowling.

If the game is being played some distance from the centre, there will be a need to check if there is a toilet in the area and if it is accessible for disabled people. A National Key Scheme Key may have to be used in some places.

Several booklets have been written on bowling and these have information on choosing equipment, holding bowls and how to play. A handbook is also available from the British Crown Green Bowling association which gives details about the rules of the game. (See Appendices)

Lawn Bowling

Bowling can be played on a lawn if there is one which is suitable to use e.g. well-cut, even, level and with enough space. The game has to be played safely and away from obstacles, shrubs and flowerbeds and also areas and paths where there may be other people.

A 'rink' or strip 3-6 metres long and 2 metres wide is recommended, though there will need to be more grass around this for any bowls which go astray.

Lawn bowls can be played in the same way as Carpet Bowls (see p111)

CHESS

Chess is a more complicated game, but it can be a useful activity in a centre where the elderly people have normal mental abilities. It can be adapted by using magnetic chessmen and boards, or the RNIB supply several different kinds of chess game for people with poor hand control, tremor or visual handicap. These include sets with pegged pieces that fit into holes in the board. Chessmen can be bought in different shapes and sizes to suit the players. In some centres a computer hame may be available, and small travelling chess sets can also be used. A non-slip mat or material placed under the board will prevent it from slipping.

Sometimes staff may be able to organise chess matches between players in the same centre or from other centres, and to award a trophy or other prize to the winner.

Since chess is quite an intricate game, it would be a good idea for staff to study a book on the subject and perhaps have a practice first before offering it to the elderly people!

Pieces on a chess board

On the top row from left to right:

Rook   Knight Bishop Queen   King   Bishop Knight   Rook

On the second row eight pawns

On the bottom row the King and Queen are in opposite places.

Moves in chess

(Black arrows are on destination squares. White arrows: the piece can go further.)

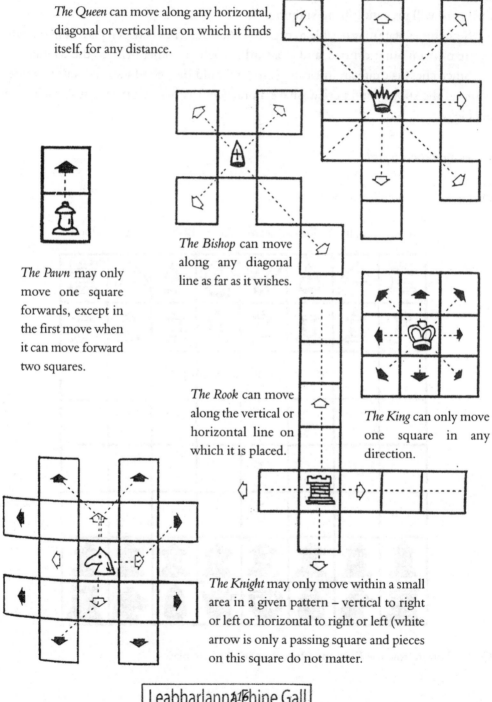

The Queen can move along any horizontal, diagonal or vertical line on which it finds itself, for any distance.

The Bishop can move along any diagonal line as far as it wishes.

The Pawn may only move one square forwards, except in the first move when it can move forward two squares.

The Rook can move along the vertical or horizontal line on which it is placed.

The King can only move one square in any direction.

The Knight may only move within a small area in a given pattern – vertical to right or left or horizontal to right or left (white arrow is only a passing square and pieces on this square do not matter.

CARD GAMES

Some elderly people enjoy playing card games and these can be an entertaining pastime in a centre. People usually know which games they want to play, have similar abilities and can organise themselves into a group, but sometimes this may not be so, and then staff will need to help to arrange a group, suggest games or provide aids or assistance.

Aids are available which will hold cards if a person is 'one-handed' or has difficulty in controlling them and some cards are adapted for people who are visually impaired, with braille or moon markings or larger symbols.

Card holders

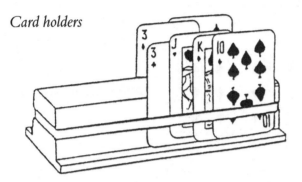

A wooden card holder with an elastic band around the centre can be used to support cards. (a plastic one without an elastic band is also available.)

An unused, upturned brush can be used to hold cards. This needs to have a flat base so that it does not 'rock'. Non-slip material can be put underneath to prevent it from slipping.

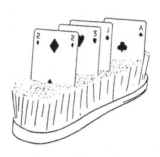

Patience Board

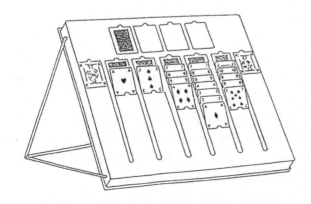

This may be needed by someone who has difficulty in controlling cards when playing Patience. It can be used either while lying down or sitting at a table.

Many card games are available, but the following two games have been found to be popular in centres:

Rummy

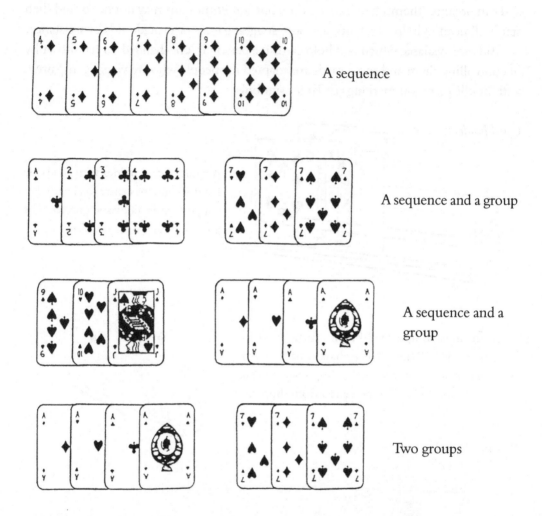

A sequence

A sequence and a group

A sequence and a group

Two groups

This game can be played by two to six players and the aim is to get a 'sequence' or a 'group' (a sequence is three or more cards which follow on in the same suit; a group is three or four cards of the same value from different suits).

After shuffling the cards, they are dealt to each person: ten cards each for two players, seven cards each for three to four players and six cards each for five or six players. The remaining cards are put into a 'stockpile' face downwards in the centre of the table, the top card is put face upwards alongside in the 'discard pile'.

Each player arranges the cards in his hand into sequences or groups. When it is his turn, he takes a card from either the discard pile or the stockpile and returns a card to the discard pile, which he does not want.

The first person to get a sequence, two sequences, a sequence and a group or two groups wins the game. In a centre it may be easier to add up the number of winning games rather than score points.

NOTE: An ace can be '1' or it can follow the King.

Whist

The first player plays a card

The second player follows suit.

The fourth player cannot follow suit and plays a 'trump' card and wins the trick.

The third player follows suit and has the highest card.

Whist is a game for four players. The aim is to get as many 'tricks' as possible (a trick is the four cards in the centre of the table).

To begin, the dealer 'cuts' the pack and the next card is the 'trump' card (a card of the same suit can beat other cards).

The dealer deals out all the cards (except the jokers) to the players who then arrange them in suits. The player on the left of the dealer starts the game and plays a card (any card) and the other players 'follow suit' (that is, play a card from the same suit). The person with the highest card wins the trick and this is put in a pile beside him. He then plays a card to start the next trick.

If a player does not have a card of the same suit, he may play another card or a trump card and win the trick. If two players play trump cards, the one with the highest card wins the trick.

Play continues until all the cards have been played. The player (or pair of players) with the most tricks wins the game.

To start again, the dealer shuffles the cards and cuts them to find the new trump card for the next game.

PATIENCE

Patience games can be played by someone who is unable to play card games with anyone else. These may be quite simple to very complicated.

If a person has difficulty in laying out cards on a table or could disturb them, he may be able to use a Patience Board.

Some easy to play Patience games –

Memory game

After the pack is shuffled, the cards are placed face downwards on a table at random. The aim of the game is for the player to try and remember where all the cards are and 'pair' them off.

At each turn, he places 2 cards face upwards, if these 'match' i.e. have the same value e.g. 2 Kings, 2 Sevens etc they are removed from the table. If not he returns them to their place again face downwards.

He continues with the game until all the cards have been 'paired off'. If there is more than 1 player, the person with the most 'pairs' wins the game.

Klondyke

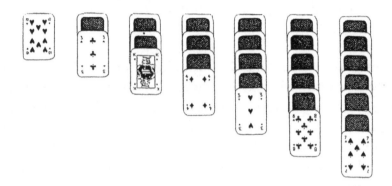

After the pack has been shuffled and jokers removed, the cards are laid out on a table in rows facing downwards with the last card in each column facing upwards.

The aim of the game is to complete four columns of cards in sequence and in alternate colours, beginning with the King at the top and ending with the Ace at the bottom.

To do this, the player takes a card from the bottom of a column or the top of the pack of cards or the top of the 'waste pile', and tries to continue a sequence – for example, Five of Diamonds on a Six of Clubs, or Queen of Hearts over a King of Spades. If a card from the top of the pack is not wanted, it is put onto the waste-pile facing upwards.

While playing, the person may move a whole sequence of cards from one column to another if this continues the sequence in the new column. (When a card or sequence is taken from a column, the next card is turned upwards.)

Royal Marriage

In the game overleaf, the Nine and Three of Clubs can be removed after the Two and Ace of Spades have been taken off the table.

This is an easy game of Patience to play. The aim is to bring the Queen of Hearts and King of Hearts cards together.

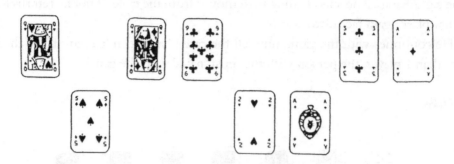

After removing the jokers, the player shuffles the cards and places the Queen of Hearts on the table at the left-hand side; the King of Hearts is put at the bottom of the pack. Taking a card from the top of the pack each time, he makes a row of cards starting from the Queen of Hearts. If a card (or pair of cards) has a card on each side of the same suit or value, the card (or cards) in between is removed from the table. The remaining cards are moved together. When the King of Hearts meets the Queen of Hearts, the game is won.

GUESSING GAMES

Blockbusters
When playing this game, questions can be chosen to suit the person being asked. Waddingtons make a small version of the game seen on television, and there was also a series of Blockbuster books.

Crosswords
Some elderly people enjoy doing crosswords. Most newspapers publish puzzles of varying difficulty, and whole books of crosswords can be bought from bookshops. These are particularly useful in a centre as they can be used by people sitting in a chair or in bed. Some puzzle magazines are published at monthly intervals and it may be worth placing a regular order for these if someone in the centre enjoys doing them.

Quizzes
These are often popular in a centre, and are a particularly good form of activity where there are plenty of able elderly people. They are easy to organise and can be made more intersting by having teams and keeping scores. Winslow Press produce a quiz book

and sets of quiz cards which can be used with elderly people. The questions are graded under different subjects.

Tell Me...

In this game someone picks a card with a question and a dial is spun to give a letter of the alphabet. When the dial stops the person has to give an answer beginning with the letter shown on the dial. As a substitute, two piles of cards can be used – question cards and alphabet cards. *Tell Me...* is made by J. W. Spears.

Trivial Pursuit

This can be a challenging game for elderly people who are able enough to take part. Questions need to be suitable for the person who is answering them and it may be helpful to have some simple ones ready in case they are needed. Both normal and children's versions are available, and the latter may be more appropriate for some elderly people.

Many other games are available in addition to the few mentioned here, but these may stimulate ideas.

If a person has poor hand control or other disabilities which prevent him from taking part in an activity, it may be possible to ask someone to help him, perhaps a relative, or else a volunteer or member of staff.

Games are usually available locally from toyshops, sports shops or stationers, but if you cannot obtain them in your area you may have to write to the manufacturers for information (see the Appendices for addresses). Some games are sold separately and boxed, while others are in a compendium. Although these are usually cheaper, the individual ones tend to be sturdier and better for withstanding the wear and tear of use in a centre.

TABLE GAMES

Beetle

In this game, each player has a pencil and paper and throws a dice in turn. Starting with six for the body, a beetle is drawn by adding a piece to the body according to the number thrown on the dice. The first person to complete the beetle wins the game.

A 3D version of Beetle is available from the RNIB for those who have difficulty in seeing a drawing or using a pencil. Beetle

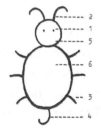

cards can also be bought and can be enlarged on a photocopier to make them easier to use.

Dominoes

This popular game is easy to play and organise. Dominoes are made in different forms to suit those who have specific difficulties – for example, coloured dominoes can be used if someone is slightly confused or has a problem in understanding numbers, and those issued by the RNIB are useful for people who have a visual problem. They have raised dots and are easy to see and hold. The RNIB also produce a wooden support for dominoes, for those who are unable to hold the pieces.

Picture dominoes, although intended for children, may be suitable for a confused elderly person who enjoys playing with them. The pictures must be appropriate for an older person.

Draughts

This is another game that elderly people may ask to play. It can be adapted by using a magnetic board and 'men' or a wooden board with sunken squares from the RNIB if a person has a tendency to knock the pieces off the board.

Ludo

'Frustration' from MB Games is an ideal game for elderly people as the dice is contained in a dome in the centre of the board – it only has to be tapped to change the position of the dice and the counters are also held in supports.

This game can be used with someone who has poor hand control and would be unable to shake a dice in the normal way.

Noughts and Crosses

This is a simple game which does not take a lot of effort but can be enjoyed by some people. It may be played with pieces, on paper or on a drywipe board though a 3D version is available – this is much more challenging as the noughts and crosses have to be played in various directions.

Scrabble

This is an interesting game for the more able as long as they have sufficient control to hold the pieces. It can be played with a 'Travel Scrabble' set, which has pieces with legs that fit into holes, or with the RNIB version which has sunken squares to take the tiles. The latter have raised markings for identification. Both these versions would be suitable for people who are likely to knock the pieces. A Giant Scrabble set from Nottingham Rehab Supplies has larger letter tiles which are easier to hold.

Scrabble can be played by several people, although one person can play on his own by trying to beat his own score for each game. Non-slip material can be used underneath the board to prevent it from slipping, or it can be put on a turntable.

OTHER GAMES

These are activities which can be done by the elderly while sitting in a circle or a group. They are easy to do and provide interest and stimulation. It is hoped that they enjoy doing them.

Balloon game
In this game the elderly have to try and knock a balloon over a 'fence' – this can be a net, a table or a group of chairs, without it dropping onto the floor. This can be a nice gentle exercise done from sitting or standing.

Basket ball
A basket or bucket is placed in the centre of a circle and the elderly people are asked to try and aim the ball into it. The person who succeeds in getting the most balls into the basket wins the game.

Capitals
Another game can be asking the elderly if they can name the capital city of different countries. It may be useful to have two lists, one easy and the other more difficult if some groups of people are slightly confused and others alert.

Crossword
For elderly people who are more alert, it may be possible to do a crossword. This can be done individually from a newspaper or a grid can be done on a blackboard copied from a book of crosswords. The clues may have to be made more simple if the group are less able.

Connect 4
In this game the elderly have to try and make a straight line of four discs horizontally, vertically or diagonally in a frame with an opponent who is trying to 'block' the line. It can be good fun and may be done from standing or sitting at a table.

Floor games
Several floor games are available from different catalogues and these are useful if you want to encourage the elderly to be more active. Winslow have a game 'Target Play' where discs are thrown over a 'target mat' to reach the 'bulls eye'.

General knowledge
General knowledge quizzes can be fun but the questions need to be suitable for the people in the group. Several quiz books are available and some of these have questions for different levels of ability.

Groups
Another game is to make a list of 'groups' and ask people if they know the ending e.g.: -

A plague of locusts	A swarm of bees	A flock of sheep
A suit of clothes	A flight of steps	A fleet of ships
A skein of wool	A bale of cotton	A bunch of fives
A pride of lions	A gang of thieves	A peal of bells

Guess the face

This can be fun. The leader collects as many pictures as possible of famous people. These may need to be faces which elderly people are likely to know from the past e.g. film stars and they are asked to recognise them.

Homes
In this game the elderly are asked if they can name the 'home' of a particular group, it may be animals, people etc. e.g.

Red Indian: Wigwam	Bee: Hive	Horse: Stable
Pig: Sty	Spider: Web	Chicken: Coop
Fox: Lair	Eskimo: Igloo	Dog: Kennel
Rabbit: Burrow	Badger: Sett	Beaver: Lodge

Hoop-la
In hoop-la the object of the game is to throw rings over a post. It could be in the centre of a circle or a straight line if done by one or two people.

Large-sized games

Sometimes games are made in a large size and these are very useful if you want people to stand or move about. They are available in several catalogues.

Memory games

Memory games are a good way of helping people to stay alert and concentrate. It can be simple objects on a tray which are covered up, card games (see p 120) or special memory games.

Musical instruments

Music can be fun in a centre and particularly if the elderly are able to play simple musical instruments e.g. drums, cymbals; triangle, tambourine, bells etc. Sometimes there may be someone who can play a piano. This activity can often be done if people are confused.

Name that tune

Music can be played and the elderly asked if they can 'name that tune'. They may be able to sing along to it. The music should be familiar for elderly people.

Offspring

In this game the group are asked if they can name the offspring of different animals. A list can be put on the blackboard or the names of animals read out e.g.

Sheep: Lamb	Seal: Calf	Deer: Fawn
Horse: Foal	Lion: Cub	Frog: Tadpole
Cat: Kitten	Goose: Gosling	Swan: Cygnet
Goat: Kid	Chicken: Chick	Fox: Cub

Parachute game

For this game the elderly are asked to sit in a circle and hold onto a 'parachute'. They can move it up and down and also balance a ball on top of it. Different activities can be done with a parachute (Nottingham Rehab Supplies have a book on 'Parachute Games')

Pass the ball

The elderly are asked to sit in a circle and to pass a ball to each other. This can be a neighbour, a person nearby or across the circle.

Places
This game can be made more interesting by getting pictures of famous places. The elderly are asked if they can name the place. Sometimes it may be possible to start a discussion about what happens there and any local items of interest.

Proverbs
This is a good game with the elderly as they are often familiar with proverbs. It is useful to have a list and to ask people if they can finish the ending. There may be a debate about what each one means. Simple proverbs can be used if the elderly are a little confused. Some examples are:

Make hay while the sun shines	Blood is thicker than water
It's no use crying over spilt milk	He who hesitates is lost
Better to be safe than sorry	Money is the root of all evil
Do not tell tales out of school	Forewarned is forearmed
Charity begins at home	Every dog has its day
Let sleeping dogs lie	Look before you leap.

(A complete list of proverbs is available in the book 'Groupwork Activities' by Danny Walsh published by Speechmark)

Quizzes
These are often popular with the elderly particularly if they are not too demanding. They can be on different subjects e.g. celebrities, songs, places etc. Quiz books are available and sometimes they have questions for different levels of ability.

Shove-halfpenny
Make or buy a shove-halfpenny board and a 'ramp' for the coin and see who can send the coin the furthest. There could be a prize for the winner.

Similes
It is useful to have a list of similes and to ask the group if they can finish each one e.g.

As mad as a hatter	As wise as an owl	As white as snow
As bald as a coot	As strong as an ox	As fresh as a daisy
As thin as a rake	As safe as houses	As dry as a bone
As good as gold	As bold as brass	As hard as nails

Sing-a-long

Sing-a-longs can be fun for elderly people particularly if they are unable to take part in other activities. They can be done without music but are better with a tape, CD or someone playing the piano. The songs should be suitable for the group who are singing and if possible songbooks or sheets can be handed around to help everyone with the words. Large print songbooks are available from the Partially Sighted Society (for address see Appendices)

Solitaire

This is a game which an elderly person can play if he is unable to join a group. To play 'patience' with cards (see p 120)

Start a tune

The person leading the group starts to sing a song and asks the elderly if they can join in. It is useful to have all the words ready in case they get forgotten!

Ten-pin bowling

This is a good game for elderly people who are able to stand safely and throw a ball or play from a chair or wheelchair. The 'pins' are laid out in a pyramid of 4, 3, 2, 1 with 1 pointing towards the player. A barrier or wall needs to be at the back of the pins to prevent the ball from rolling away.

(To find out more information about the above games please see: – 'Creative Games in Groupwork' by Robin Dynes published by Speechmark. 'Groupwork Activities' by Danny Walsh published by Speechmark)

(It may be possible to play some of these games with elderly people who are confused)

WORD-FINDING GAMES

These can be popular with the elderly and are also easy to organise. They can be done using a board in front of the group or at a table using a piece of paper.

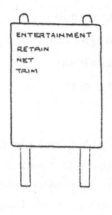

1 **Words in a word**
A long word is written on the board and the group are asked to make as many words from it as possible.

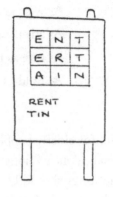

2 **Grid**
A nine-letter word is written into a grid and people are asked to think of as many words as possible from the letters in the grid.

3 **Broken-line game**
In this game the leader thinks of a word and this is written onto the board in broken lines. People are asked to think of a letter which may fit into the word.

4 **Mixed-up word**
A word is jumbled up and written on the board and people are asked if they recognise it. Words need to be easy and not too long.

Equipment

To play some games, it is useful to have a board in front of the group, such as a blackboard or flip-chart or a 'drywipe' board. It should be possible to obtain one of these from a local shop, but if not a supplier may be able to give details (see Appendices for addresses).

To avoid buying a chalkboard, blackboard paint can be used on a piece of wood. Boards can be held by hand or propped against a wall on a table, but it is easier if they can be fixed on a wall or supported on a stand.

JIGSAWS

Some elderly people enjoy making up jigsaw puzzles. These may be quite small – 32 pieces – or very large, with perhaps 4,000 pieces or more. Wooden pieces are easier to hold and more suitable for those who have difficulty in holding card pieces, and the ones with the larger pieces are also easier to see if a person has a visual problem. Care should be taken to ensure that any puzzles used have pictures which are suitable for elderly people.

Once a suitable jigsaw has been chosen, you will need to find a jigsaw board or tray – this should be non-slip or have a lip round the edge to prevent any pieces falling off. It must be larger than the jigsaw. If a tray is not available (catering trolley trays can sometimes be used), you may be able to make one from a piece of wood with beading round the edge (see below). Sometimes a lap tray can be used if the jigsaw is quite small.

Jigsaws can be made up by a person on his own or may be a joint venture and completed by several people, perhaps working at different times. In this case the jigsaw can be left on a table in an area where it will not be disturbed.

Finished jigsaws can be dismantled for future use or they may be glued onto a piece of hardboard and hung on a wall. To do this, cover the completed jigsaw with a piece of thin wood and holding the wood and tray very firmly, turn the jigsaw upside down so that the picture is facing downwards. Remove the tray and using a general purpose glue such as Uhu, cover the entire surface of a piece of hardboard and press the glued side onto the back of the jigsaw. Leave to dry and then turn the jigsaw face upwards again. (A special glue for jigsaws can also be used to hold the pieces together.) Screw fittings onto the back of the hardboard and hang on a wall. Some jigsaws may be framed like a picture.

Making a jigsaw tray

Cut a piece of plywood or hardboard larger than the size of jigsaw to be used.

Useful sizes are:
46 x 30.5cm for the smaller puzzles

61 x 46cm for
53 x 40cm puzzle

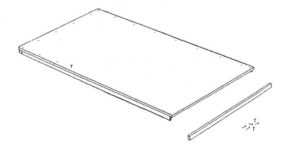

91.5 x 61cm
76 x 53cm puzzle

Measure four pieces of beading to fit around the edge. Glue these onto the plywood or hardboard with wood adhesive. When dry hammer in panel pins or small nails from underneath, ensuring that these are level with the wood. (Jigsaws can be stored on jigsaw trays when not in use.)

Using a 'Porta-Puzzle' board

It may be easier to rest the 'Porta-Puzzle' board on a lap tray when it is being used in a chair.

A jigsaw can be made up on a 'Porta-Puzzle' board. This has a non-slip surface and also hinged flaps, which are folded over the jigsaw when it is not in use and it has to be carried around or stored away. (Pieces left on the side flaps have to be put onto the main part of the board so that the jigsaw is held securely.)

It may be used at a table, in bed or on the lap of a person sitting in a chair. The board should fit comfortably in between or on top of the arms of the chair and sometimes a smaller board may have to be used or it can be put on a lap tray.

The Porta Puzzle board is available in 3 sizes: – 530 by 405mm, 760 by 530mm and 910 by 660mm and can be obtained from some shops which supply jigsaws. (See Appendices for address)

Aid

Insert a hat pin or normal pin through a piece of cork.

A person with limited hand function may be able to use this to 'stab' the cardboard pieces.

SPECTATOR SPORTS

Sometimes elderly people are unable to join in an activity, but they may get a lot of enjoyment from visiting a sports ground, watching it on television or listening to the radio.

In a residential centre, this can give someone an interest and particularly if they are able to use a radio and headphones in a day room or have their own TV and keypad so that the right channels can be chosen.

Cricket

Cricket grounds usually have access for disabled people and places where matches can be viewed from a wheelchair, most have toilets for the disabled and refreshment areas which can be used by people with a disability.

Cricket is a leisurely game which is often enjoyed by the elderly – a magazine on the sport is available for anyone who would like to know more about the game.

Football

Most football clubs now have facilities for disabled visitors and provide refreshment areas and toilets which can be used by people in wheelchairs, though it is worthwhile asking staff first if these are available before making any arrangements.

At some grounds, disabled people have to book in advance and there may be stewards who will give assistance – a commentary service is available in some places.

Golf

Golf is a leisurely sport which can sometimes be watched on television. If a person has details about the course, this can make it more interesting.

A magazine can be bought which gives information about the game.

Horse-racing

Watching horse-racing either on television or at a racecourse is often an enjoyable pastime and particularly if the elderly person is able to put on a bet!

Most racecourses do have facilities for disabled people with special car parking and viewing areas and access to toilets and refreshment places, though staff will probably need to know in advance about the visit.

Following this sport can also be fun for someone who may be confined to bed or in a chair and can watch TV or listen to the radio.

Bets can be made through a betting shop either in person or by telephone using a Delta or Switch card number or a credit account. Some betting agencies also have a 'phonabet' scheme whereby money is left at the betting shop and deductions are made from this for the bets.

Details about forthcoming races and events are available in the 'Racing Post' and other newspapers.

Motor sports

Racing circuits usually have facilities for the disabled and races can often be viewed from the parking area.

If a person is unable to visit a race track, he may be able to watch it on television. Several magazines are available which give details about the different events and other information.

Snooker

Another interesting activity which can be seen at a snooker hall or on TV.

Many games are shown on television and news items etc, can often be found on TELETEXT.

Information about access to sports grounds and other facilities are included in the book 'Spectator Sports – A guide for disabled people' from RADAR.

9 OTHER ACTIVITIES

BAKING

This can be an enjoyable activity for elderly people in a centre. It gives them a sense of purpose, and an opportunity to show their skill and contribute to the running of the centre.

Cakes and buns are popular favourites, although some people may be able to attempt more ambitious ideas. If a group of people want to take part in the activity, it may be possible to split it up so that different people are doing different activities – one person weighing ingredients and others mixing them, and so on. Others may be willing to do the more simple tasks like washing up or laying the table.

If the people are quite fit they may be able to work in a normal kitchen, but others may prefer to sit at a table if a low work surface is not available in the kitchen. In some centres it may be safer and more convenient to keep the elderly people away from the kitchen and to use a table in another room.

Aids are available if anyone needs to use them. These include non-slip mats, bowl supports and recipe book holders, as well as adapted cutlery, utensils and kitchen furniture. Elderly people with a particular disability may be able to buy aids to suit their own needs – for example, the RNIB has a range of aids for people with a visual handicap and some of these can be used in the kitchen. A local Disabled Living Centre is likely to have a display of kitchen aids and may also have the services of an occupational therapist who can give advice and assistance.

In all activities, elderly people need to be supervised, particularly in kitchen areas where there are equipment and utensils. Before using these, some elderly people may need a demonstration on the correct use so that they can work with them safely. In some instances it may be necessary to check the Health and Safety policy.

It can be an interesting project to encourage the elderly people to contribute recipes etc. towards a cookery book, especially if they are long-stay residents, and it can help towards fund-raising in the centre. Any activity that helps in the running of the centre should be voluntary and should complement the work already being done by the staff.

BIRDWATCHING

Birdwatching can be an interesting hobby if an elderly person is able to see birds or listen to their sounds. It may be done while lying in bed or sitting in a chair (if the window is at a convenient height and overlooking the garden) or sitting outside on a bench or in a wheelchair. It can also be done from a car or minibus though some elderly people may be able to walk in a park, join a ramble or visit a nature reserve and perhaps even attend an evening class or course. Local birdwatching groups sometimes arrange talks, outings and other events.

If there is a garden or patio, it is useful to have a birdtable and birdbath though these often need to be off the ground and away from any hiding places where there may be cats. Nesting boxes should be in a quiet area, which is away from the sun in the middle of the day. Anything used in a garden has to be in a place where it can be seen easily by the elderly people and also accessible for staff who have to fill it. Window bird feeders are available which use suction cups to attach to the outside of a window, though it may be easier to use a normal feeder if it can be suspended securely from the fitments on the window opening. (Gardmans 'tubes' of bird seeds can be used to fill the feeder.)

To attract birds into the garden it may be worthwhile having a variety of plants with berries which they like to eat e.g. Berberis, Cherry, Cotoneaster, Hawthorn, Holly, Japonica and Rowan and also plants which attract insects. Some birds enjoy scraps of food which have been put out on a tray or nuts hanging in a bird feeder.

Binoculars are a useful aid for birdwatching and particularly for elderly or disabled people who are unable to get close enough to see the birds. Lightweight and easy to hold ones are available and some have a connection which can be attached to a tripod. Sizes 8 by 30 or 8 by 40 are usually recommended for birdwatching.

If a person has his own binoculars he may be able to adjust these to suit his own needs. This can be done by closing his right eye and moving the 'centre wheel' to focus the left lens and then closing his left eye and altering the adjustment around the right lens. After this only the centre wheel has to be changed when he is trying to focus on the birds. If binoculars are shared in a centre, they may have to be adjusted each time they are used. Someone with glasses may find it easier to fold back the 'eyecups' on the binoculars.

Binoculars can be fixed on a tripod or held against or on top of a firm object e.g. a wall to keep them steady. A person in a wheelchair may be able to rest his elbows on the armrests while he holds the binoculars. Aids can be bought if someone has difficulty in holding them.

Different books have been written on birdwatching and these can often be obtained

from a local library though sometimes it may be possible for a librarian to bring them into the centre. The Royal Society for the Protection of Birds (RSPB) have leaflets on how to identify and look after garden birds and also a list of nature reserves which can be used by disabled people. They publish a quarterly magazine for members and have films, tapes and videos. The BBC has compact discs of bird sounds which are available from Video Plus Direct (for addresses see Appendices)

CENTRE NEWSLETTER

It may be useful to have a centre newsletter, or a group of centres may share one. This can be helpful in passing on information to the elderly people, as well as encouraging them to take a more responsible part in the running of the centre. It can be organised by a member of staff or a group of elderly people may work together to produce it. The kind of activities involved can include collecting and editing information, typing, writing articles, drawing sketches or cartoons, compiling crosswords, puzzles or competitions, having a question and answer column, finding out what is on or available in the area, noting any local items of interest, and encouraging other elderly people to contribute; lastly there is the duplicating and distributing of the newsletter. A photocopying machine can be invaluable for copying or enlarging a newsletter, or it can be done on a computer using a printer though it may be possible to use carbon paper if a machine is not available. A newsletter may be produced monthly or quarterly or less often, depending upon the amount of information available and the needs of the people using the centre.

Sample of some of the items which may be included in a centre newsletter.

Centre Newsletter

Spring 1990   No. 3

Dear All,

　　We hope that you enjoyed the recent visits to Skegness and Derbyshire and that you are looking forward to the holiday in the Summer. Thank you for all the contributions to the Newsletter – any reader's letters not included in this issue will be mentioned in the next one,
　　Editor.

From the staff...

The plans for the new extension to Highfields Centre have been agreed so there may be some disruption during September when one of the day rooms will need to be closed.

Harvest Festival

The Minister will be holding the Harvest Festival earlier this year – can you let staff know if you want to contribute anything towards this.

Smile awhile

At a recent nativity play in the village, one little girl was heard to exclaim that she was taking the part of Joe Smith.

Concert

A concert has been arranged at the Highfields Centre on Monday, July 7th at 3 p.m. – can you let staff know if you would like to go so that transport can be arranged.

Snooker

The Snooker Competition will be held in the Broad acres Centre during May – please let Mrs Griffeths know if you will be entering this year.

Library Service

Good news for readers! The Librarian will be visiting again during March to change the books in all the centres – please let her know if there are any particular books which you would like to read.

Crossword

Joe Crosby has compiled a new crossword (overleaf) – answers to the last crossword are also included.

What's on

There will be an 'Old Time Music Hall' at the Alhambra Theatre on May 14th at 7p.m. Facilities are now available for wheelchair users so if you would like to go, please can you let staff know by April 10th.

Minibus

It has been agreed that all the centres are to contribute towards a minibus which can be used for outings.

Films

A list of forthcoming films at the local cinema has been put up on all the noticeboards.

Reader's letters...

Dear Editor,

I would like to ask why the Domino Match was cancelled this year. I really enjoy playing the game and was very disappointed at the news, Phyllis Johnson.

(We regret that the match had to be cancelled, Mr. Jeffries the organiser had to leave suddenly during August and we were unable to find a replacement in time. The match for this year will be held as usual)

Roadworks

A warning to residents who may have a visual problem – the pavements on Walkley St and Howarth Row leading to the park will be blocked during August, please can you use the opposite pavement if you are using this route.

Friends of Broadlands Centre

The Friends of Broadlands Centre would like to thank everyone who contributed to their fund-raising event in October.

A centre newsletter can also be used to include a programme of activities for the week or month ahead so that elderly people can choose which ones they would like to attend.

COLLECTING COINS, POSTCARDS, STAMPS

Collecting things can be fun and sometimes people enjoy doing this in a centre. It may be done by someone confined to a room or by a group of people with a similar interest.

A member of staff may need to be involved to give support and also bring in things from outside.

Popular items to collect are photographs, coins, postcards, stamps and magazine or newspaper cuttings. Some of these can be glued into a scrapbook, while others may need a special album.

It is an inexpensive hobby and can often give stimulation to someone who enjoys looking through papers and magazines etc.

Sometimes people are able to join clubs or societies and receive information by post or it may be possible to start a group in the centre or between centres.

Coins
Coins are usually kept in a 'coin album' and magazines are available which give details about the different kinds of coins and their value. Some people do this as an 'investment' but in a centre it may just be for general interest.

Postcards
Postcards can be fixed into a scrapbook with 'photo corners' or glue, though it is better if they are put into a postcard album. Family or friends can be asked to send them and sometimes it may be possible to get postcards of people or old scenes which are familiar to the elderly person.

Stamps
Stamp-collecting is a popular hobby and particularly as there can be a wide choice of stamps – very little is needed except an album, hinges, tweezers and perhaps also a magnifying glass.

Stamp albums do vary in price and it may be worthwhile looking around to see which ones are most suitable for elderly people – albums with 'strips' are easier to use if someone has difficulty in handling hinges and pages which show pictures of the different stamps are helpful for people who want to know what to collect and where to put them.

Stanley Gibbons have a catalogue which gives useful information about their range of albums, accessories, stamps and publications and the British Philatelic Bureau has stamps, first-day covers and presentation packs (see Appendices.)

If several people are interested in stamp-collecting, it may be possible to form a group in the centre or between centres where they can exchange stamps and perhaps also information and magazines.

COMMITTEES

A committee representing the elderly people can be very helpful in running a centre, especially if the members are alert and able and the meetings are well organised and active. A staff member may need to be included to guide the meetings and also to organise certain aspects of an activity, such as arranging transport, sending for tickets or checking that amenities are suitable for disabled and elderly people.

The committee can be structured like any other, with a chairman, a secretary to take notes and a treasurer who will keep a record of any funds. If there are any particular groups of people attending the centre, such as those with a visual impairment or an ethnic minority, they should be asked to put forward a representative. An agenda may be drawn up or meetings may be organised informally – points to raise from people attending the centre, or information which the staff would like to pass on. Meetings may also include discussion about events to be organised and any other points of interest.

The kinds of activity in which the committee can become involved include making arrangements for outings and collecting names and payments; asking for slide, film and video shows and suggesting speakers for talks and demonstrations. They may also assist staff with other activities e.g. organising bazaars, sales of work, jumble sales, fundraising and other events.

Perhaps one of the most useful functions of a committee is that the members can collect information, views and criticisms from the people attending the centre and pass these on to the staff. This is especially helpful in a centre which has large numbers of people attending on different days, and only a limited number of staff.

When a committee is formed there is likely to be a need for some form of rules, so that guidelines can be followed in electing members and setting a limit to the term of office. Meetings may be held regularly or irregularly depending on the needs of the centre and as often as necessary. In a day centre a monthly meeting may be appropriate, while in a long-stay unit a quarterly meeting may be enough. If the centre has a different group of people attending on each day of the week, a separate committee may be needed for each day.

Some elderly people may have a particular skill which they can use on a committee, and if this can be utilised it will be rewarding for them as well as helpful to the centre. They may be good at organising other people, or be able to lead a meeting, take notes, liase with staff, be responsible for money, or simply have a capacity to contribute in some way.

The need for an elderly people's committee will vary from centre to centre. In some it may be very successful and make a useful contribution to the running of the centre, while in others it may be difficult to organise, particularly if the elderly people are frail or confused, or unable to tackle the work involved.

CONCERTS

Concerts play an important part in the life of a centre, particularly if the elderly people are resident there. They range from formal ones given by professional musicians to quite informal productions organised by local volunteers; they may even be put on by the staff or the elderly people themselves.

A concert may include music played or sung, songs in which the audience can take part, comedy, drama, stories, poems, monologues or whatever talents are available. It may be organised around a theme such as old time music hall, or it may be held to celebrate a special occasion.

It helps to get to know local people or groups who can provide entertainment – a choir, an ensemble, a band or orchestra, bellringers, dancers, a school, college or church group, a comedian, a magician, a pianist, a singer, or perhaps a mixture of several different talents. After a while you will get to know which acts the elderly people enjoy most and can ask them to visit again.

The facilities needed for a concert vary according to the nature of the performers and the size of the audience. You will probably need a large room, a piano, chairs (with arms) for the elderly people, access for wheelchairs, extra seating for visitors and somewhere for the entertainers to use as a dressing room. The room should be well lit, heated and have sufficient ventilation. You may also need additional items such as songbooks and music.

In any activity involving groups of people it is essential to ensure that there is easy access for everyone – for the elderly people to leave the room if necessary and for staff to reach someone who needs their help. This may mean additional aisles through the audience (wide enough for wheelchairs) which are essential if everyone has to be evacuated in an emergency.

Before the concert begins, staff may like to say a few words of introduction, perhaps giving the names of the entertainers, they may also like to call for a vote of thanks afterwards.

After the concert refreshments may be provided, these are usually welcomed by the entertainers and the audience and also give everyone a chance to meet each other. Some entertainers may charge a fee for their services while others will ask for nothing. As most entertainment does involve cost of some kind, it is worthwhile having a fund so that money is available for this purpose.

EXHIBITION, SALE OF WORK OR FAIR

An exhibition or sale of work

This can be an important event in the life of the centre, it gives the elderly people an interest and a reason for collecting or making items during the year.

If work is to be exhibited, staff should try to make a special occasion of it with prizes and perhaps a person of some standing to present them. A local photographer can be commissioned to take photographs of the exhibits or presentations which can later be enlarged and hung in the centre.

Preparation for this kind of activity requires a lot of effort on the part of the staff, but usually it is all worthwhile, a day for the elderly people to enjoy each year.

When planning an exhibition or sale of work you should consider the following points: the size of the room or rooms where the work will be displayed; the size and number of tables and chairs and any other displays; the space required for the visitors and the elderly people (who may be in wheelchairs); and fire regulations. Posters for display in local shops and public buildings will have to be made or copied, as well as signs for the different crafts and labels for each item. If these are not being judged, the person's name can be used; otherwise they can be numbered. These labels must be fixed securely as items can easily be lost or mislaid. Award cards can be bought and prizes will also need to be purchased. You may want to have cups or shields which would need engraving.

Tables and other surfaces look better if covered with sheets, material or paper and display boards can be covered with material and placed on top of the tables to hold exhibits. On some surfaces a staple gun or drawing pins can be used to attach coverings. The exhibits can be pinned onto the material on the display boards or hung or laid on the table. Try to show them off to their best advantage – badly made items can often be camouflaged. Staff may also like to trim the tables with decorations.

On the day itself activities should take place at pre-arranged times – for example, judging at 1pm, opening at 2pm and the presentation of prizes at 3pm.

Additional attractions such as background music and refreshments can all help to make it an enjoyable day. If refreshments are provided, these may need to be served in a separate room or area.

A fair

This is a bigger event to organise and usually needs a group of staff to plan it well beforehand. As well as some of the activities mentioned above, there may be games and fund-raising stalls such as a white elephant stall, a second-hand book stall, a plant stall, a cake stall, a toy stall and so on. You could also have a tombola session, raffles, guessing the weight of a cake and much more. When organising a fair you may have to recruit relatives, carers and volunteers as well as staff to man the stalls, supervise the elderly people, organise the refreshments, collect and count the money, relieve others on duty and do any other tasks that may be necessary. You may also have to decide whether to hold the fair inside or outside; if you choose out-of-doors you will need to make some provision for rain.

Refreshments can be more ambitious and you may be able to ask a local band to come and play, all adding to the atmosphere of the occasion. Bunting displayed around the centre will help to set the scene and will also advertise the event.

If the elderly people can become involved in the preparation and organising of activities it will not only be helpful to you but will give them a sense of purpose.

FLOWER ARRANGING

This interesting and absorbing craft can offer much variety depending upon the skill and enthusiasm of the arranger. Many books have been written about flower arranging and these include useful instructions not only on fresh and dried flowers, but also on flowers made out of other materials such as silk, plastic and paper. Some also include information about pressed flowers for anyone who is interested in making pressed flower pictures or greetings cards.

Some elderly people may be able to attend flower arranging demonstrations organised by a local flower arranger's society or to visit a national show. Some may even be able to attend evening classes and learn from trained teachers how to create professional and artistic arrangements. The National Association of Flower Arrangement Societies (NAFAS) is involved in organising shows and demonstrations and also issues a quarterly magazine giving useful information and listing forthcoming events. If any elderly people are unable to leave the centre a local flower arranger may be willing to visit occasionally and give a demonstration.

Basic equipment for the craft could include a selection of different containers, pin holders to support the flowers and special 'putty' to hold them in place, 5cm fine gauge wire netting, 'oasis' which can be soaked in water (for fresh flowers), 'oasis' which does not need soaking (for dried flowers) and clippers. Those who are more ambitious and want to make an arrangement around a theme may need additional materials for their display.

Once the flowers have been bought (or picked from the garden) and the equipment obtained, the flower arranger has everything she needs to enjoy a light hobby that would be ideal for someone unable to attempt more strenuous activities. The finished arrangements will also make the centre a more attractive place and give pleasure to other elderly people using it, including those with a visual impairment who may be able to feel and smell the flowers. If an arranger has the use of only one hand the container can be placed on a non-slip mat before the arrangement is started.

For those interested in pressing flowers, a complete flower pressing kit is available from Specialist Crafts and the same company also makes flower presses in small, medium and large sizes. It is also possible to achieve excellent results by placing the flowers between the pages of an old telephone directory with a heavy weight on top of it.

INDOOR GARDENING

If someone enjoys gardening but is unable to go outside, indoor gardening may be the answer. This is an enjoyable pastime and can be made more interesting by having different kinds of plants and a range of containers around the centre – potted plants on a shelf or window ledge (or in a window box), in a plant stand or in a large container on the floor. It may also be possible to install a bottle garden or a terrarium (fishtank garden).

Some of the activities demand skill and you may have to split these up so that they can be done by different people. One person can choose seeds or take cuttings, another can prepare the soil or containers, another set the seeds or the cuttings and yet another can feed and care for the plants afterwards. Indoor gardening can be done by someone who has limited vision or from a wheelchair and it is ideal for an elderly person who lacks the stamina to attempt outdoor gardening.

The equipment used need not be expensive and is usually available from the local garden centre. You will need clay or plastic plant pots (6.5cm, 9cm, 13cm and 18cm have been found to be the most useful sizes), drip saucers, fertiliser, pest killer, potting compost, secateurs, string, stakes, an old fork and spoon, a soft sponge for washing leaves, a mister for spraying plants and a watering-can. Small lightweight watering-cans are now available with a broad, stable base and those with an extended spout are particularly useful for people in wheelchairs. If someone is liable to spill the water, it may be better to use a mister or a container with a lid – an old teapot is ideal for this purpose. Visitors may be willing to bring in plant pots and other equipment that they no longer need.

Other aids include a fitted tray on a wheelchair, non-slip mats under the containers, labels with braille markings and tools with adapted handles. If a worktop is being used, it may need to be secured, and you should also check that it is at a convenient height for people who are sitting down or in a wheelchair.

Flowering plants which may be grown indoors include African violet, azalea, begonia, Busy Lizzie, flowering cacti, campanula, chrysanthemums, cyclamen, perlargonium, poinsettia and primula. Non-flowering foliage plants may also be grown. Someone who cannot see easily will appreciate scented plants such as gardenia or jasmine.

Some ideas for indoor gardening

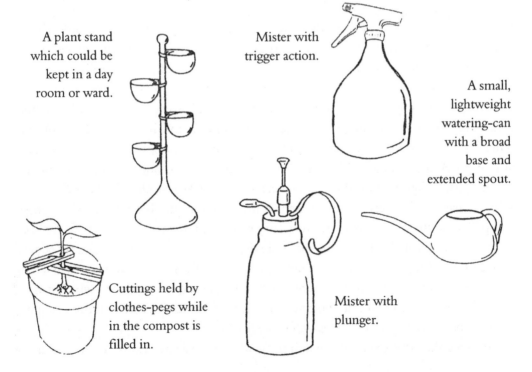

A plant stand which could be kept in a day room or ward.

Mister with trigger action.

A small, lightweight watering-can with a broad base and extended spout.

Cuttings held by clothes-pegs while in the compost is filled in.

Mister with plunger.

Preparing a bottle garden

1
Pour an even layer of gravel through a stiff paper tube or funnel

2
Pour a layer of potting compost over the gravel

3
Using a spiked stake to manoeuvre a plant into position.

OUTDOOR GARDENING

Outdoor gardening can be an interesting and absorbing hobby for anyone who is sufficiently able, and the flowers and produce can be used to benefit the centre. If possible the garden should be near to the centre where facilities are available, and so that staff can keep an eye on the elderly people and be on hand if any problems arise.

It is possible to plan a garden to suit the needs of elderly people, and information can be obtained on the subject so that any alterations can be made. Horticultural Therapy and the Disabled Living Foundation will both supply helpful leaflets and advice (see Appendices for addresses.) Non-slip ramps can be built (a minimum incline of 1:12,) paths that are wide, firm and level enough to take wheelchairs, broad, shallow steps so that a walking frame can be used on them, and handrails can be fitted by ramps and paths and in other areas where they may be needed. Raised edges on paths help to prevent wheelchairs from slipping off, and raised beds will be easier for elderly people who find bending down difficult. These can be specially designed and constructed in brick, stone, concrete or wood, or they may be tall, portable containers, which can be set up in various places around the garden or on paved areas. If a garden is not available, hanging baskets or window boxes will provide interest.

If a greenhouse is to be included in the garden or on a paved area, it, too, will need to be suitable for elderly people, allowing access for wheelchairs and fitted with worktops that are firm, strong and of a convenient height. A water or electricity supply may be an advantage and perching stools can be provided for those who are unable to stand for long periods. When siting a greenhouse look for a sunny area, not too exposed, which has good access to supplies and is preferably near to the centre. If space is limited, a lean-to greenhouse may still be useful, particularly if easy access is required.

Some centres may have a special room or a shed which can be used to store tools, equipment and materials. This should not be too far away from the garden so that the elderly people can reach it easily.

Benches can be positioned in various places so that people can rest or view the garden. Any structures in the garden should be safe and strong, since elderly people may need to hold on to them for support.

Gardening can be enjoyed by people with several different handicaps, and also by those whose sight is failing, although it may need special adaptations for a person who has severe visual impairment.

Equipment

It is usually possible to obtain most pieces of gardening equipment such as long-handled tools, from your local garden centre, although occasionally you may have to contact the firms manufacturing particular items (for suppliers see Appendices.) The two pieces of equipment below have been found especially useful with elderly people.

Perching stool

Kneeler

This is a high seat which may have an adjustable seat as well as a backrest and arms.

This can be used as a stool or a kneeler and can be made from wood or tubular steel. It is useful for an elderly person who can sit or kneel while working.

Long-handled tools

Easy reach pruning gun

Baronet pruner and flower gatherer

Thickening a tool
handle with Rubazote

Gardenmate wheelbarrow

Working in a
raised flower bed

Using a small two-wheeled
wheelbarrow – this can also be used
if a person has a walking stick.

A lightweight and well balanced
watering can

LIBRARY

A Library service is essential in a centre where there may be a number of elderly people
who enjoy reading.

Those who ask for a book are usually able to manage on their own, although some
will need aids and assistance.

A library service is easy to maintain once started and can normally be managed by a volunteer or perhaps by one of the elderly people themselves. The local public library may be happy to exchange books at intervals and may give advice on setting up a service and keeping records of books loaned out, returned and requested. Books can be stored in a cupboard or on shelves, and a book trolley is useful in a centre where some of the elderly people may not be mobile. It can also be used to store magazines, talking book tapes, reading aids, newspapers and any other material that needs passing round. Book trolleys need to be robust and may have to fit in with the rest of the furniture in the centre. They can be ordered from hospital, library and school suppliers.

Some elderly people have difficulty in reading the print in normal books and may manage better with large print books, which are published by several companies (see Appendices). Magnifying aids can also be supplied to make the print easier to see. People with a more severe visual impairment may enjoy talking books. These are taped versions of well-known books and can be bought or borrowed from the local library. Most can be played on a normal cassette player, but some require special equipment for which there is usually a charge. The cassettes can be played to a group of people, or used in individual cassette players with headphones.

If any other aids are needed, an occupational therapist maybe able to give advice, or a librarian or the local Disabled Living Centre may provide ideas. Bookrests are available for use in bed or in a chair, and special tables are also manufactured. Some of these have a ledge and are adjustable in height and angle, others have swivel legs which are useful for fitting around or in between chairs. Pageturners come in various forms to cope with degrees of disability; a rubber thimble on a finger, or on the end of a stick or headpointer is the simplest form, but there are also simple pageturners for people with some hand function, and more expensive electronic models for those who have difficulty using their hands at all.

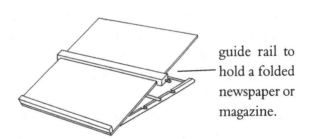

guide rail to hold a folded newspaper or magazine.

An open-ended table which slides easily under chairs. Both height and angle are adjustable.

'Eschenbach' bookrest

Some people enjoy being read to from newspapers, magazines or books, and volunteers can be asked to do this. Other elderly people like reading aloud, and a reading circle can be a pleasant pastime, each person having a copy of the same book and reading a passage in turn until the chapter or story is finished. The local library may be able to supply several copies of large print books of the same title for use in such groups, or the book can be passed round the group. In some centres it may be worthwhile ordering daily newspapers or subscribing to magazines if the elderly people enjoy reading them.

MUSIC

Music can provide a lot of fun in a centre, particularly for confused elderly people who may be unable to take part in many of the other activities. Sing-songs, perhaps one of the most enjoyable pastimes can entertain the most restricted person, especially if the songs are familiar to him.

Sung music is usually easier to follow if the words are written down or displayed, and if they can be blown up on a photocopier the elderly people will be able to see them more easily. The staff should know the words and tunes so that they can help everyone along. In general the music will need to be clear, lively and louder than normal to cater for those who are partially deaf.

If there is a piano in the centre it will add to the fun if a member of staff, a volunteer or perhaps one of the elderly people can play, particularly if some of the elderly people can dance with each other or with the staff. In centres where the people are more physically able it may be possible to organise socials and other events.

Sometimes people will offer to visit the centre to play musical instruments, and some of the elderly people may be able to join in and either take a turn on these instruments or use instruments available in the centre, such as tambourines, triangles, drums and so on. More able people may provide their own entertainment.

In some centres it may be necessary to provide some kind of entertainment throughout the day, such as television, radio, a hospital radio system or a music centre. The latter can be invaluable for a long-stay resident, enabling staff or the elderly people to put on records, tapes, compact discs or the radio, whichever is preferred. Individual radio-cassettes with headphones can be bought for use in areas where people may want to be quiet while others can enjoy a tape of their choice.

A good selection of singalong videos, tapes, sheet music and song books is available in shops or by mail order, including large print song books for those with less than perfect sight.

MUSIC AND MOVEMENT

In a centre an activity like this can provide beneficial exercise for elderly people, as well as encouraging them to be sociable.

When arranging the group you will need to look at the numbers of people involved in relation to the size of the room and the number of staff available. You must also consider their disabilities and abilities and ensure that the activity is appropriate for them and the skills of the staff leading the group. Between seven and fifteen people has been suggested as suitable for a music and movement session, although the numbers may vary depending on the independence of the elderly people and the amount of supervision and assistance they need. Before asking them to take part in the group find out whether they have a condition that could be affected by the exercises or whether their behaviour is likely to interfere with the running of the group.

It is usual for the elderly people to be sitting down during the session as there is always a risk that some people may fall if they do exercises while standing. Ordinary chairs can be used, although chairs with armrests are safer. People in wheelchairs can normally join in.

The group is arranged in a circle or semi-circle with the chairs spaced at least two armlengths apart so that no one gets injured. The leader can sit inside the circle or in front of the semi-circle to demonstrate the exercises. How much space is required will depend on the number of people taking part, and you should check the fire regulations to make sure that you are not exceeding the maximum number permitted for safety. You will need one member of staff to lead the group and a second on hand to assist the elderly people and take anyone out if necessary she can also help in an emergency. Additional staff may be needed if the elderly people are very dependent.

The exercises should be well planned and suitable for people who are sitting down. Take care that an elderly person is not asked to do an exercise that is beyond his ability. It is a good idea to start with breathing and limbering up exercises before building up to more strenuous activity. Simple, slow exercises can be alternated with quicker ones demanding more agility, and different parts of the body can be used in consecutive exercises so that the elderly people do not tire too easily. You can include exercises involving the head, neck, shoulders, elbows, wrists, hands and fingers, and also the trunk, hips, knees, ankles, feet and toes, although hip exercises will be limited if a person is sitting down. Household and other tasks can be used to make the session more interesting and to encourage a wider range of movement – for example, pretending to wipe the door, wall, ceiling and so on. A cloth can be used to add authenticity to the movement.

You can also make use of equipment such as balls, beanbags and hoops; these can be passed from person to person, across the circle or can be part of an individual exercise. You may need special equipment for anyone who has a specific disability – for example, padded balls with bells for partially sighted people.

Any music for the group should be planned in advance so that it fits in with the exercises and the session runs smoothly. You may need to make special tapes for the different sessions by taking music from other tapes and records and recording it in sequence onto a blank tape. The rhythm and tempo of the music should be appropriate for each exercise, and you will find that music that has a definite beat and is not too fast is most suitable for elderly people. They will respond best to music that is familiar to them – indeed, if you can use old time songs you may get them to join in with the singing.

(It is important that an elderly person should not be asked to try and do an activity that could aggravate his condition or cause stress or discomfort. In a music and movement group this might happen if his shoulder is stiff and painful as a result of a stroke. If you are in doubt about what to do, ask a doctor or therapist for advice before starting the session.)

OUTINGS

In some centres outings may be arranged – these are particularly important in residential homes. They provide an opportunity to meet other people as well as to take part in activities outside the centre. You could organise visits to a church, a pub, shops, a community centre, the cinema, theatre or concert hall, a park or recreation area, a tea-room or a café; or to take part in a bowling match, to go fishing, attend a further education course or to visit an exhibition, craft fair or flower festival. Outings lasting several hours could be arranged to the coast or countryside, or a holiday lasting several days or longer. Sometimes exchange plans can be made, whereby elderly people from one centre can exchange for a short period with those living in another centre.

Before making any arrangements, you need to consider the following points: -

- Who would like to go?
- Are they well enough?
- Have they had a 'risk assessment'?
- Can they travel easily, safely and without discomfort?
- Where would they like to go?

- Will the elderly people be paying their own expenses or will these come out of centre funds?
- Is transport available and is it suitable for people in wheelchairs?
- Has the vehicle been well-maintained?
- Is the driver over 21 with two years driving experience and does he have a suitable licence for the vehicle?
- Are there enough escorts?
- Are experienced staff going on the outing?
- Will tickets be required?
- Is the chosen destination suitable for elderly and disabled people – for example, could a person in a wheelchair reach and use all the facilities such as toilets and refreshment areas?
- If the visit is outside – have other arrangements been made if the weather is unsuitable?
- Should anyone be notified about the visit?
- Are there adequate stopping places on the way with access to toilets for disabled people?
- Is a National Key Scheme key available? (Keys can be obtained from local Social Services Departments or from RADAR who also have a list of toilets.)
- Are any additional items needed – for example, First Aid, medication, tissues, blankets, towels and perhaps urinals with lids?

Many factors may need to be considered, but it is as well to plan in advance so that everything runs smoothly on the day.

If people are being taken to the theatre, cinema or concert hall in wheelchairs you will need to find out if there is an entrance which is level or has a ramp and if the facilities inside are convenient for someone in a wheelchair e.g. wider doorways, enough space to manoeuvre the wheelchair, lift or ramp to other floors and level access into the auditorium and disabled toilets. When making the booking staff there may want to know how many people will be in a wheelchair as there is usually a restriction on the number of wheelchairs which can be allowed inside a building. During the performance staff from the centre may have to sit near to the elderly people so that they can give assistance if needed.

In some centres the elderly people may be able to help organise the outing by taking names of people who would like to go and any payments required.

Take care when choosing escorts if they are not staff members. They should be no younger than 18 and no older than 65 and you should ask for references if they are not relatives or friends of the elderly people. Some centres require escorts to sign a form saying that they will be responsible for the person in their care during the day. They should be fit, caring, responsible people and remember that they may need training in the care and handling of an elderly person. You may also have to show them how to use a wheelchair and other equipment correctly. How many escorts you take on the outing will depend on the abilities of the elderly people themselves. If most of them are in wheelchairs or have mobility problems, then one escort per person is likely to be needed; if the elderly people are more able you will need fewer escorts, but you should ask the elderly people to stay in groups so that they can be supervised more easily.

When going on an outing you have to choose a suitable vehicle and check that a lift or ramp is available if it will be carrying wheelchair-users. You will also need wheelchair tie-down and passenger restraint systems (see Outdoor Transport.)

Elderly people need adequate clothing when they go out, and this is particularly important for people in wheelchairs who may have to sit for long periods in cold and draughty areas. Special clothing is available for this purpose, made in waterproof or shower-proof materials.

You can find out about access from RADAR who supply lists and you can simplify the problem of getting the elderly people from the vehicle to the place you are visiting by using the Blue Badge parking scheme (previously the Orange badge parking scheme.) This national scheme allows disabled drivers and passengers to park in areas normally prohibited to vehicles, such as free and unlimited parking at on-street parking meters and in time-limited waiting areas and for 3 hours on single or double yellow lines if there are no double white lines in the centre of the road. Anyone using this scheme must park safely and not cause an obstruction. The scheme is available to severely disabled people who use a motor vehicle supplied for disabled people by a Government Health Department, receive the higher rate payment of the mobility section of the Disabled Living Allowance, are registered blind, have a severe upper limb disability affecting the ability to use a steering wheel or have a permanent and substantial disability which causes very considerable difficulty in walking (For more information see Appendices)

If an outing is planned from a day centre you will need to make arrangements for returning the elderly people to their homes at night, and remember that, whatever activity you choose, you must follow the guidelines laid down by the organisation responsible for the centre.

RECALL

Many elderly people enjoy reminiscing and a recall group can be a good way for them to get together and have a discussion, particularly if a member of staff can lead the group.

Initially you might try a session with a fairly small group of people who are alert and can see and hear, although later on you may be able to include more people and those with disabilities.

To start the session an old time music tape or record will help to get people in the mood and put them at ease with each other. The Education Department of Help the Aged has a selection of tapes, slides and notes which correspond with different periods from the First World War onwards. These will help to remind the elderly people about the different events in their childhood and will also help an inexperienced group leader. After showing the slides you can put a blank tape on the tape recorder to record the discussions that follow. This will help to remind the leader of what has been said and may provide ideas for later discussion – it serves as a reminder of where the previous discussion ended. Sometimes elderly people may make comments during the showing of the slides and the leader can take notes of these.

You can also get the talk flowing by producing objects from the past, or pictures of them, or by showing mementoes or photographs of past happenings. Sometimes reading from old newspapers will revive memories and encourage people to contribute to the discussion. It is also fun to compare prices and fashions with those of the present day.

To stimulate interest, your local library may be able to provide information about local history, and may have pictures and objects which can be shown to the group. The librarian may even be willing to organise a recall session herself. Local antique and junk shops, too, may have commonplace articles that can be used in discussions.

Equipment you could use might include a slide projector, a screen or plain wall and a tape recorder. A double tape recorder would enable you to transfer information from one tape to another.

The group leader should try to acquire a reasonable knowledge of the subject to be discussed before starting the session, as she may need to interject ideas when there is a lull in the conversation.

RELIGIOUS SERVICES

Some elderly people may be able to visit a local church or chapel, but if this cannot be done it may be possible to arrange a service in the centre. A minister or priest from one of the main Christian denominations can be asked to officiate, and if the service is kept simple it is usually acceptable to most of those who attend. If you have people from other faiths attending the centre, it may be possible to arrange services for them also.

The service can be held on a Sunday or another day of the week, and may be weekly, monthly or less frequent, depending on the availability of the minister. You may be able to organise a rota of ministers who will visit at different times.

Arrangements for a service can be quite simple – a quiet room or area, a piano, a table with a cloth, and a standing cross and flowers if these are available. If you have no piano in the centre, the minister may be able to bring a portable organ and perhaps an organist and members of his own congregation to help with the singing. You will need to provide the pianist or organist with a music edition of the hymnbooks distributed to the elderly people, and have spare hymnbooks for staff and visitors. If some of the elderly have a visual impairment, you may need to buy large print hymnbooks.

Often the minister will organise his own order of service, although he may ask if any of the elderly people would like to take part by singing a hymn, reading from the Bible, playing the piano or contributing in some other way.

If you serve refreshments after the service you will help to make it more of a social occasion and will enable the elderly people to meet the visitors.

Harvest Festival

This is organised in the same way as any other service, except that fruit and vegetables will have to be bought or brought in by the elderly people or their visitors. These can be arranged on plates and put on the improvised altar. The minister will usually give a harvest service, and you should check that you have the appropriate music and hymns. Advertise the service in advance so that the elderly people have an opportunity to make a contribution. Any produce can be given to the elderly people afterwards or used in the kitchen.

This service is well worth organising and the elderly people enjoy making a contribution.

Carol service

This is usually a simple service to organise and need not involve a minister of the church. It is often linked to other Christmas celebrations and all you will need are carol sheets that can be easily read by elderly people. If an accompanist and music are available the service will be more enjoyable. To create an atmosphere you could sing carols round a crib or have one or more candles in the centre of the room.

10 APPENDICES

SOME CONDITIONS WHICH MAY BE FOUND IN ELDERLY PEOPLE

Angina
In angina, the nutrition to the heart muscle is limited. This may be due to narrowing of the blood vessels feeding the muscle, or to disease or degeneration of the heart itself. The condition is often associated with high blood pressure and rheumatic heart disease, and is found in those who overwork and lead stressful and anxious lives.

Arteriosclerosis
Hardening of the arteries, especially the middle coat of the arteries, often associated with high blood pressure. It generally affects all the arteries and can be hereditary, although it is known to be associated with anxiety, high tension of living and other stressful conditions. It usually refers to hardening of the smaller arteries.

Atherosclerosis
Degeneration which occurs mainly on the inner lining of the larger arteries. It usually happens in later life and tends to increase with advancing age. It is sometimes associated with an excess intake of animal fats. In cerebral atherosclerosis, when the arteries of the brain are affected, there may be giddiness, loss of memory and mental changes.

Bronchitis
Inflammation of the lining of the bronchi (tubes in the lungs), which may be acute or chronic. Acute bronchitis is usually caused by bacteria and occurs most frequently in winter and foggy weather. It is especially common among the elderly. Chronic bronchitis is a condition which generally arises in people who are heavy smokers or have lived and worked in areas with severe atmospheric pollution. It manifests itself usually in the colder months, although some elderly people may have it all year round. The main symptoms are a cough, shortness of breath, especially on exertion, and wheeziness in the chest. It may be associated with heart failure. Cyanosis or blueness in the extremities may be present and there may also be oedema (collection of fluid in the tissues). Elderly people with this condition should be encouraged to keep warm and avoid smoking and getting chills.

Cataract
The lens inside the eye is transparent and the images seen are normally focused onto the retina at the back of the eye. In cataract the lens becomes partially or completely opaque and the person loses his ability to see. In the elderly this may be due to degeneration or it can be caused by injury or it may be found in a person with diabetes. An operation can be performed to improve the condition.

Diabetes   In diabetes the body's ability to regulate the amount of glucose entering the blood becomes impaired. This causes thirst, loss of energy, loss of weight and frequent passing of urine. If the condition is not treated, a person may become unconscious. Diabetes may be treated by giving a low carbohydrate diet, a diet and insulin tablets or a diet and insulin injections, depending upon the severity of the condition.

Embolism   An embolus is an obstruction in a blood vessel. It may be part of a blood clot, a bubble of air, a globule of fat or other material. It can occur in any part of the body, but is most serious when it happens in the brain (cerebral embolism,) heart (coronary embolism) or in the lungs (pulmonary embolism.)

Emphysema   Tends to occur in the elderly and is frequently associated with chronic bronchitis and asthma. The air sacs in the lungs become overdistended with air, and degeneration in their walls means that they have lost their elasticity. It is often connected with smoking. The symptoms are mainly those of chronic bronchitis.

Glaucoma   Occurs when there is increased pressure inside the eye. This happens when there is a build up of fluid which is unable to drain away naturally. The condition can put pressure on the optic nerve and cause blindness.

Heart failure   Occurs when the amount of blood pumped out by the heart is too small for the needs of the body. This failure can occur in the left ventricle or chamber (left ventricular failure) or in the right ventricle (right ventricular failure.)

High blood pressure   High blood pressure (hypertension) is quite a common condition, in which the blood pressure is higher than normal. The walls of the arteries may also have become degenerated and thickened, and the strain on the heart to provide the body with an adequate blood supply may be greater than normal. Congestive cardiac failure may result from this condition.

Hypothermia   In hypothermia the temperature of the body falls to 95° – 96°F (35° – 35.5°C) or below and a thermometer which will give a lower reading has to be used. (Normal temperature is 98.4°F (37°C.) This may happen if someone falls and is unable to get up again, lives in a cold place, moves very little or is confused. It is a serious condition and the person needs to see a doctor or be admitted to hospital. Wrap him in a blanket, but do not expose him to direct heat e.g. a hot-water bottle or fire.

Low blood pressure Low blood pressure (hypotension) may occur naturally in some elderly people or it may be a consequence of rest or fatigue. In certain cases it may occur with a heart condition or other complaints. A person with diabetes may suffer from postural hypotension and feel faint when he tries to stand upright. In hypotension there is a limited supply of blood to the brain.

Myocardial infarction Also known as coronary heart disease, coronary arterial disease or coronary thrombosis. The myocardium is the middle lining of the heart wall and it receives its blood supply from the coronary arteries. If the walls of these vessels become thickened and the arteries become narrow and a clot forms and blocks the flow of blood, the tissue beyond the blockage is said to be an 'infarct' or dead tissue. A person with this condition may have previously suffered from an attach of angina.

Multiple sclerosis Multiple sclerosis (MS) or disseminated sclerosis is a chronic and progressive disease which may cause a variety of symptoms, e.g. weakness, numbness, eye conditions, etc. It affects the nerves of the brain and spinal cord where patches of scarring (sclerosis) are formed. These are usually scattered and can lead to symptoms which are unpredictable. The disease is usually discovered in younger or middle-aged people, so an elderly person with the disease is likely to have had it for some time. Remissions can occur from time to time, but are usually followed by relapses.

Osteoarthritis Osteoarthritis (or osteoarthrosis) is a common complaint in the elderly and is caused by 'wear and tear' in the joints. It usually affects those taking the weight of the body, e.g. hips, knees or spine, and a person may complain of pain and stiffness, particularly early in the morning. He may also find that the joints 'give way' as the muscles around them become weaker through lack of use. Elderly people with this condition should be encouraged to move their joints and not remain in one position for too long.

Osteoporosis Occurs when there is a lack of calcium in the bones. People with this condition tend to become shorter, and deformities and sometimes fractures can develop. A spinal jacket may be worn to prevent deformities in the spine. A diet rich in protein and calcium is recommended.

Paget's disease Results in some of the bones becoming spongy and thickened and is most obvious in the skull and bowing of the legs. Deafness may occur in some cases.

Parkinson's disease	This condition was named after a doctor who first described it in 1817. It affects the part of the brain involved with movement and a person with the disease may show fixed posture, shuffling gait, dribbling, expressionless face, difficulty in swallowing and in starting and performing movements, tremor, slurred speech and slowness of movement. The blank expression on the face can give the illusion that he is unaware of what is happening and staff need to respond to him normally and wait for his reactions. Drugs can be given to relieve symptoms.
Pneumonia	Means inflammation of the lungs and may be 'lobar pneumonia' or 'bronchopneumonia'. In lobar pneumonia one or more lobes of a lung are affected. This tends to be an acute condition and can end in a crisis if it is not treated. It affects the ait sacs in the lung, but not the bronchi or larger tubes. Bronchopneumonia affects the bronchioles or smaller tubes and can be patchy and affect both lungs. It may be secondary to another condition such as bronchitis, and occurs more often in the elderly who maybe suffering from general debility and other conditions.
Rheumatoid arthritis	An inflammatory condition affecting the smaller joints, e.g. of the hands or feet, although later it may spread to the larger joints. It causes pain, swelling and stiffness in the joints and in severe cases deformaties such as 'drifting' of the fingers. People with rheumatoid arthritis should try to avoid putting strain on their joints or keeping them in one position for too long. Different methods or the use of aids can make the performance of activities easier and gentle exercises can help to strengthen muscles and tendons around a joint. Splints are sometimes used to reduce deformities.
Thrombosis	Occurs when a blood clot blocks an artery or vein. It may be a coronary thrombosis (in the heart), cerebral thrombosis (in the brain) or a deep venous thrombosis (DVT) in the leg. In elderly people a DVT may happen after an operation, when bandages are applied too tightly to the leg, or may be the result of immobility.

ABBREVIATIONS

AIDS	– Acquired Immune Deficiency Syndrome
BASE	– British Association for Service to the Elderly
CCF	– Congestive Cardiac Failure
COAD	– Chronic Obstructive Airways Disease
COSHH	– Control of substances hazardous to health
CPA	– Centre for Policy on Ageing
CPN	– Community Psychiatric Nurse
CRUSE	– Organisation for counselling the bereaved
CSV	– Community Service Volunteer
CTA	– Community Transport Association
CVA	– Cerebral vascular accident (stroke)
DIAL (UK)	– Disablement Information and Advice Lines
DLF	– Disabled Living Foundation
DPTAC	– Disabled Persons Transport Advisory Committee
DVT	– Deep venous Thrombosis
GP	– General Practitioner
HSE	– Health and Safety Executive
MAVIS	– Mobility Advice and Vehicle Information Service
ME	– Myalgic Encephalomyelitis
MIND	– National Association for Mental Health
MND	– Motor Neurone Disease
MS	– Multiple Sclerosis
M&SRC	– Mobility and Specialised Rehabilitation Centre
NAPA	– National Association for Providers of Activities for Older People
NCV	– National Centre for Volunteering
OA	– Osteoarthritis
OT	– Occupational Therapist
PHAB	– Physically Handicapped and Able-Bodied
POSSUM	– Patient-operated electronic selector mechanism
PT	– Physiotherapist
RA	– Rheumatoid Arthritis
RADAR	– The Royal Association for Disability and Rehabilitation
RCN	– The Royal College of Nursing
REMAP	– Rehabilitation Engineering Movement Advisory Panels
RNIB	– Royal National Institute for the Blind
RNID	– Royal National Institute for Deaf People

ROSPA   – Royal Society for the Prevention of Accidents
RVS   – Royal Voluntary Service
SAGA   – Holidays for the elderly
TIA   – Transient ischaemic attack
TSO   – The Stationery Office

PREFIXES AND SUFFIXES

A-	—without	Ex-	—away from	-oid	—like
-able	—able to	Fore-	—in front of	-ology	—study of
-aemia	—blood	Gastro-	—stomach	-oma	—tumour
-aesthesia	—sensibility	Glyco-	—sugar	-opia	—eye
-al/-an	—pertaining to	-genic	—origin of	Ortho-	—straight/normal
-algia	—pain	-graphy	—recording	Oro-	—mouth
Ambi-	—on both sides	Haema/haemo	—blood	Os-	—bone/mouth
An-	—absence of	Hemi-	—half	-ose	—sugar
Ante-	—before	Homo-	—same	-osis	—condition
Anti-	—opposite to	Hydro-	—water	Osteo-	—bone
Bi-	—two	Hyper-	—excess	-ostomy	—to form an opening
Brady-	—slow	Hypo-	—below		
Broncho-	—connected with the lungs	-iasis	—condition of	Oto-	—ear
		In-	—in	-otomy	—incision of
-cardial	—heart	Inter-	—between	-ous	—having nature of
Cardio-	—heart	Intra-	—within		
Cerebro-	—brain	-itis	—inflammation of	Pachy-	—thickness
Co/Con-	—together	-kinesia	—movement	Pan-	—total
De-	—away/ from/reversing	Laryngo-	—larynx	Para-	—partial/beside
		-logy	—study of	-paresis	—weakness
-derm	—skin	Macro-/Mega-	—large	Patho-	—disease
-desis	—to bind together	Mal-	—abnormal	-pathy	—disease
Dis-	—against	Medi-	—middle	Ped-	—child/foot
Dys-	—difficult/ painful/abnormal	Meta-	—between	Per-	—by/through
		Micro-	—small	Peri-	—around
-ectomy	—removal of	Multi-	—many	Pharyngo-	—pharynx
En-/End-/Endo-	—in/ into/within	My/myo	—muscle	-phesia	—speech
		Neo-	—new	Phlebo-	—vein
Ent-	—within	Nephro-	—kidney	-plasty	—to form
Epi-	—outside	Neuro-	—nerve	-plegia	—paralysis
-esis	—action/process	Oculo-	—eye	Pleuro-	—covering of the lung

Pneumo-	—air/lung	-sclerosis	—hardening	Thrombo-	—blood clot
-pnoea	—breath	Semi-	—half	Thyro-	—Thyroid gland
Poly-	—many	Socio-	—sociology	-tomy	—incision of
Post-	—after	-stomy	—to form	Tracheo-	—wind pipe
Pre-/pro-	—before		an opening	Trans-	—across
Pseudo-	—false	Sub-	—below	Tri-	—three
Psycho-	—mind	Supra-	—above	-trophy	—nourishment
Quadri-	—four	Syn-	—union	Ultra-	—beyond
Re-	—again	Tachy-	—fast	Uni-	—one
Retro-	—backward	Tarso-	—foot	-uria	—urine
Rhin-	—nose	-therapy	—treatment	Vaso-	—vessel
Sclero-	—hard	Thoraco-	—chest	Veno-	—vein

USEFUL ADDRESSES

Government departments

Public Enquiries Unit, Department of Health, Richmond House, 79, Whitehall, London SWIA 2NS

Tel: 020 7210 4850   Textphone: 020 7210 5025   Fax: 020 7210 5952

Web: www.gov.uk/government/organisations/department.of.health

Department of Transport (DfT), Great Minster House, 33, Horseferry Road, London SWIP 4DR
Enquiry Line: 0300 330 3000   Web: www.dft.gov.uk

Department of Work and Pensions (DWP), Caxton House, Tothill Street. London SWIH 9NA   Web: www.dwp.gov.uk

Disability Benefits.   Web: www.gov.uk/browse/disabilities

Disabled Persons Transport Advisory Committee (DPTAC), Great Minster House, 33, Horseferry Road, London SWIP 4DR
Email: DPTAC. Enquiries@dft.gsi.gov.uk Web: www.dptac.gov.uk

Forum of Mobility Centres, c/o, Providence Chapel, Warehorne, Ashford, Kent TN26 2JX
Tel: 0800 559 3636   Email: mobility@rcht.cornwall.nhs.uk

Health and Safety Executive
Tel: 0300 003 1747   Web: www.hse.gov.uk

Medicines and Healthcare Products Regulatory Agency (MHRA), 151, Buckingham Palace Road, Victoria, London SWIW 9SZ
Tel: 020 3080 6000   Fax: 0203 118 9803
Email: info@mhra.gsi.gov.uk   Web: www.mhra.gov.uk

Motability.
Tel: 0300 456 4566   Web: www.motability.co.uk

Service Personnel and Veterans Agency, Norcross, Thornton Cleveleys, Lancashire FY5 3WP
Helpline: 0808 1914 2 18   Web: www.veterans-uk.info/

Professional bodies

British Association of Art Therapists, 24-27, White Lion Street, London N1 9PD
Tel: 020 7686 4216   Fax: 020 7837 7945
Email: info@baat.org   Web: www.baat.org

British Association for Counselling and Psychotherapy, BACP House, 15, St John's Business Park, Lutterworth, Leicestershire LE17 4HB
Tel: 01455 883300   Text: 01455 560606   Fax: 01455 550243
Email: bacp@bacp.co.uk   Web: bacp.co.uk

British Association of Social Workers, 16, Kent Street, Birmingham B5 6RD
Tel: 0121 622 3911   Fax: 0121 622 4860
Email: england@basw.co.uk   Web: www.basw.co.uk

British Dietetic Association, (BDA), 5ᵗʰ Floor, Charles House, 148/9, Great Charles Street, Queensway, Birmingham B3 3HT
Tel: 0121 200 8080   Fax: 0121 200 8081
Email: webmaster@bda.uk.com   Web: www.bda.uk.com

British Association for Music Therapy (BAMT), 24-27, White Lion Street, London N1 9PD
Tel: 020 7837 6100
Email: info@bamt.org   Web: www.bamt.org

Ceretas (previously the British Association of Domiciliary Care), 21, Regent Street, Nottingham NG1 5BS
Tel: 0115 959 6130   Fax: 0115 959 6148
Email: admin@ceretas.org.uk   Web: www.ceretas.org.uk

Chartered Society of Physiotherapy, 14, Bedford Row, London WCIR 4ED
Tel: 020 7306 6666
Email: enquiries@csp.org.uk   Web: www.csp.org.uk

College of Occupational Therapists, 106-114, Borough High Street, Southwark, London SE1 1LB
Tel: 020 7357 6480
Email: Reception@cot.co.uk   Web: www.cot.org.uk

Health and Care Professions Council (HCPC), Park House, 184, Kennington Park Road, London SE11 4BU
Tel: 0845 300 6184   Fax: 020 7820 9684
Email: registration@hcpc-uk.org

Royal College of Nursing (RCN), 20, Cavendish Square, London WIG ORN
Tel: 020 7409 3333   Web: www.rcn.org.uk

Royal College of Speech and Language Therapists (RCSLT), 2, White Heart Yard,
London SE1 INX
Tel: 020 7378 1200
Email: info@rcslt.org   Web: www.rcslt.org

Society of Chiropodists and Podiatrists, 1, Fellmonger's Path, Tower Bridge Road,
London SE1 3LY
Tel: 020 7234 8620
Email: reception@scpod.org   Web: www.feetforlife.org

Voluntary Organisations

Attend (previously the National Association of Hospital and Community Friends),
11-13, Cavendish Square, London WIG OAN
Tel: 0845 4500285   Fax: 0207 3072571   Web: www.attend.org.uk
Carers Trust (previously Crossroads Care and the Princess Royal Trust for Carers),
32-36, Loman Street, London SE1 OEH
Tel: 0844 800 4361   Fax: 0844 800 4362   Web: www.carers.org/merger

Carers UK, 20, Great Dover Street, London SE1 4LX
Tel: 020 7378 4999   Advice Line: 0808 808 7777
Email: adviceline@carersuk.org   Web: www.carersuk.org

Community Service Volunteers (CSV), 237, Pentonville Road, London N1 9NJ
Tel: 020 7278 6601   Fax: 020 7833 0149
Email: information@csv.org.uk   Web: www.csv.org.uk

Community Service Volunteers Retired and Senior Volunteer Programme
(CSV/RSVP), 237, Pentonville Road, London N1 9NJ
Tel: 020 7643 1385
Email: rsvpinfo@csv.org.uk   Web: www.csv-rsvp.org.uk

Citizens Advice, Myddelton House, 115-123, Pentonville Road, London N1 9LZ
Web: www.citizensadvice.org.uk

Cruse Bereavement Care, PO Box 800, Richmond, Surrey TW9 1RG
Tel: 020 8939 9530   Helpline: 0844 477 9400
Email: helpline@cruse.org.uk   Web: www.cruse.org.uk

National Association for Voluntary and Community Action (NAVCA), The Tower, 2,
Furnival Square, Sheffield S1 4QL
Tel: 0114 278 6636   Textphone: 0114 278 7025   Fax: 0114 278 7004
Email: navca@navca.org.uk   Web: webedit@navca.org.uk

National Council for Voluntary Organisations (NCVO), Society Building, 8, All Saints
Street, London N1 9RL
Tel: 020 7713 6161   Fax: 020 7713 6300
Email: ncvo@ncvo.org.uk   Web: www.ncvo-vol.org.uk

Royal Voluntary Service (previously WRVS), Cardiff Gate, Beck Court, Cardiff Gate
Business Park, Cardiff CF23 8RP
Tel: 0845 608 0122   Web: www.royalvoluntaryservice.org.uk

Organisations concerned with elderly people

Age UK (previously Age Concern and Help the Aged), Tavis House, 1-6, Tavistock
Square, London WC1H 9NA
Advice line: 0800 169 6565

Age Scotland, Causewayside House, 160, Causeway, Edinburgh EH9 1PR
Helpline: 0845 125 9732   Web: www.ageuk.org.uk/scotland

Age Cymru, Ty John Pathy, 13/14, Neptune Court, Vanguard Way, Cardiff CF24 5PJ
Tel: 029 2043 1555   Advice line: 08000 223 444
Web: www.ageuk.org.uk/cymru

Age Northern Ireland, 3, Lower Crescent, Belfast BT7 1NR
Advice line: 0808 808 7575   Web: www.ageuk.org.uk/northern-ireland

Centre for Policy on Ageing, 25-31, Ironmonger Row, London ECIV 3QP
Tel: 020 7553 6500   Web: www.cpa.org.uk

Counsel and Care (Turn2us), Twyman House, 16, Bonny Street, London NW1 9PG
Advice line: 0845 300 7585
Email: advice@counselandcare.org.uk   Web: www.counselandcare.org.uk

National Association for Providers of Activities for Older People (NAPA), 1st Floor,
Unit 1, Fairview Industrial Estate, Raans Road, Amersham HP6 6JY
Tel: 020 7078 9375   Fax: 01494 726752
Email: info@napa-activities.co.uk   Web: www.napa-activities.co.uk

The Third Age Trust, U3A, The Old Municipal Buildings, 19, East Street, Bromley
BR1 1QE
Tel: 020 8466 6139   Web: www.u3a.org.uk

Residential Care/Housing

The Abbeyfield Society, St Peters House, 2, Brickett Road, St Albans, Herts. AL1 3JW
Tel: 01727 857536   Fax: 01727 846168
Email: post@abbeyfield.com   Web: www.abbeyfield.com
Association of Retirement Housing Managers (ARHM), c/o EAC, 3rd Floor, 89, Albert
Embankment, London SE1 7TP
Tel: 020 7463 0660
Email: enquiries@arhm.org   Web: www.arhm.org

Care Quality Commission, National Customer Service Centre, Citygate, Gallowgate,
Newcastle-upon-Tyne NE1 4PA
Tel: 03000 616161   Fax: 03000 616171   Web: www.cqc.org.uk

Elderly Accommodation Counsel (EAC), 3rd Floor, 89, Albert Embankment, London
SE1 7TP
Tel: 0800 377 7070   Advice line: 020 7820 1343   Fax: 020 7820 3970
Email: info@firststopadvice.org.uk   Web: www.eac.org.uk

Help the Hospices, Hospice House, 34-44, Britannia Street, London WC1X 9JG
Tel: 020 7520 8200   Fax: 020 7278 1021
Email: info@helpthehospices.org.uk

Leonard Cheshire Disability, 66, South Lambeth Road, London SW8 1RL
Tel: 020 3242 0200   Fax: 020 3242 0250
Email: info@1cdisability.org   Web: www.1cdisability.org

National Disabled Persons Housing Service Ltd., 17, Priory Street, York YO1 6ET
Tel: 01904 653888
Email: info@hodis.org.uk   Web: www.hodis.org.uk

Registered Nursing Home Association (RNHA), John Hewitt House, Tunnel Lane,
Off Lifford Lane, Kings Norton, Birmingham B30 3JN
Tel: 0121 451 1088   Freephone: 0800 0740 194   Fax: 0121 486 3175
                         Web: www.rnha.co.uk

Relatives and Residents Association, 1, The Ivories, 6-18, Northampton Street. London
N1 2HY
Tel: 020 7359 8148   Helpline: 020 7359 8136   Fax: 020 7226 6603
Email: info@relres.org   Web: relres.org

Sue Ryder Care, First Floor, 16, Upper Woburn Place, London WC1H OAF
Tel: 020 7554 5900
Email: info@suerydercare.org   Web: www.suerydercare.org

United Kingdom Home Care Association (UKHCA), Group House, 52, Sutton Court
Road, Sutton, Surrey SM1 4SL
Tel: 020 8288 5291   Helpline: 020 8661 8188   Fax: 020 8288 5290

Disability

Capability Scotland, Head Office, Westerlea, 11, Ellersly Road, Edinburgh
EH12 6HY
Tel: 0131 337 9876   Textphone: 0131 346 2529
Email: capability@capability-scotland.org.uk   Web:www.capability-scotland.org.uk

Disability Information Scotland, Hays Business Centre, 4, Hay Avenue, Edinburgh
EH16 4AQ
Tel: 0131 669 1600
Email: info@update.org.uk   Web: www.update.org.uk

Disabled Living Foundation, Ground Floor, Landmark House, Hammersmith Bridge Road, London W6 9EJ
Tel: 020 7289 6111   Helpline: 0300 999 0004
Email: info@dlf.org.uk   Web: www.dlf.org.uk

Disability Rights UK (previously RADAR), 12, City Forum, 250, City Road, London ECIV 8AF
Tel: 020 7250 3222
Email: enquiries@disabilityrightsuk.org   Web: www.radar-shop.org.uk

Enabling Partnership. Enham, Enham Place, Enham Alamein, Andover, Hampshire SP11 6JS
Tel: 01264 345800   Web: www.enham.org.uk

National Back Exchange (NBE), Linden Barns, Greens Norton Road, Towcester, Northampton NN12 8AW
Tel: 01327 358855   Web: nationalbackexchange.org
Email: admin@nationalbackexchange.org

Physically Handicapped and Able-Bodied (PHAB), PHAB Office, Summit House, 50, Wandle Road, Croydon, Surrey CRO 1DF
Tel: 020 8667 9443   Fax: 020 8681 1399
Email: info@phab.org.uk   Web: www.phab.org.uk

Rehab UK, Brain Injury Services, London Brain Injury Centre, 21, St Thomas Street, London SE1 9RY
Tel: 020 7378 0505   Fax: 020 7403 4219   Web: www.rehabuk.org

Remap (Head Office), D9, Chaucer Business Park, Kemsing, Sevenoaks, Kent TN15 6YU
Tel: 0845 130 0456   Fax: 01732 760204   Web: www.remap.org.uk

Rica (RICA), (Research Institute for Consumer Affairs), GO3, The Wenlock, 50-52, Wharf Road, London N1 7EU
Tel: 020 7427 2460   Fax: 020 7427 2468
Email: mail@rica.org.uk   Web: www.rica.org.uk

Scope, 6, Market Road, London N7 9PW
Tel: 020 7619 7100   Tel: 0808 800 3333
Email: response@scope.org.uk   Web: s www.scope.org.uk/dial

United Kingdom Disabled People's Council (UKDPC), 27, Old Gloucester Street, London WC1N 3AX
Tel: 020 8522 7433   Web: www.ukdpc.net

Disabled Living Centres

These centres give information and advice on a wide range of aids and equipment for elderly people and those with disabilities. In some centres an appointment may be necessary, so it is advisable to telephone before visiting.

Assist UK (previously the Disabled Living Council) DLCC, Redbank House, 4, St Chad's Street, Manchester M8 8QA
Tel: 0161 832 9757   Web: www.assist-uk.org

Inspire Community Trust, 20, White Hall Lane, Bexley, Kent DA8 2DH
Tel: 0203 045 5100   Minicom text: 0132 334 716
                    Web: www.inspirecommunitytrust.org

Assist Birmingham Centre (ABC) for Independent Living, St Mark's Street, Springhill, Birmingham, West Midlands B1 2HU
Tel: 0121 464 4942   Textphone: 0121 464 7565   Fax: 0121 464 4944
Email: assistbirminghamcentre@birmingham.gov.uk

Disabled Living Centre, British Red Cross, 35, Skirbeck Road, Boston, Lincolnshire PE21 6DG
Tel: 0845 054 7171   Web: www.redcross.org.uk

Brighton and Hove Daily Living Centre, Montague House, Montague Place, Brighton, East Sussex BN2 1JE
Tel: 01273 296132
Email: dlc@brighton-hove.gov.uk   Web: www.brighton-hove.gov.uk

The Vassall Centre, Gill Avenue, Bristol, Avon BS16 2QQ
Tel: 0117 965 9353   Fax: 0117 965 3652
Email: mobserv@thisisliving.org.uk

The Opal, Assessment and Demonstration Centre, Unit 17-18, Bishopgate Business
Park, Widdrington Road, Coventry CV1 4NA
Tel: 024 7678 5252   Fax: 024 7625 6583
Email: occupationaltherapy@coventry.gov.uk

Croydon Equipment Solutions Ltd. 28, Boulogue Road, Croydon, Surrey CRO 2QT
Email: aztec.centre@croydon-equipment-solutions.com

South Yorkshire Centre for Inclusive Living (SYCIL), Disability Resource and Training
Centre, M+M Business Park, Doncaster Road, Kirk Sandall, Doncaster DN3 1HR
Tel: 01302 892 949   Text: 01302 329 788   Fax: 01302 885 023
Web: www.sycil.org.uk

Dudley Assisted Living Centre, 1, Jacknewell Court, Dudley WV14 9LP
Tel: 01384 813 695   Fax: 01384 813 696
Web: www.dudley.gov.uk

Dundee Independent Living Centre, Unit T, Charles Bowman Avenue, Claverhouse
West Industrial Estate, Dundee, Scotland DD4 9UB
Tel: 01382 307631   Fax: 01382 502263
Email: dilc@dundeecity.gov.uk

Disability Resource Centre, Poynters House, Poynters Road, Dunstable, Bedfordshire
LU5 4TP
Tel: 01582 470 900   Fax: 01582 470 959
Email: information@drcbeds.org.uk   Web: www.drcbeds.co.uk

East Sussex Disability Association, 1, Faraday Close, Hampden Park, Eastbourne, East
Sussex BN22 9BH
Tel: 01323 514 515   Textphone: 01323 514 502   Fax: 01323 514 501
Email: info@esda.org.uk   Web: www.esda.org.uk

Lothian Independent Living Centre, Smart Centre, Astley Ainslie Hospital, Grange Loan, Edinburgh EH9 2HL
Tel: 0131 537 9190   Fax: 0131 537 9200
Email: dlc@nhslothian.scot.nhs.uk

Moray Resource Centre, Maisondieu Road, Elgin, Morayshire IV30 IRX
Tel: 01343 559 461   Textphone: 01343 551 376   Fax: 01343 542 014
Email: info.ilc@moray.gov.uk

Poole Centre ILC, New Grosvenor Road, Ellesmere Port, Cheshire CH65 2HB
Tel: 0151 337 6399

British Red Cross Disabled Living Centre, Swaby Resource Centre, Gainsborough, Lincolnshire DN21 2TJ
Tel: 01427 816500

Web: www.redcross.org.uk

Dundas Resource Centre, Oxgang Road, Grangemouth, Scotland FK3 9EF
Tel: 01324 504 311   Fax: 01324 504 312   Web: www.falkirk.gov.uk

British Red Cross Disabled Living Centre, Unity House, Grantham, Lincolnshire NG31 7UH
Tel: 0845 054 7171
Email: granthamdlc@redcross.org.uk   Web: www.redcross.org.uk

Halton Independent Living Centre, Colliers Street, Runcorn, Halton, Cheshire WA7 1HB
Tel: 01928 563 340   Fax: 01928 582 950

Hartford Independent Living Centre, 5, Hartford (Business Centre), Chester Road, Hartford CW8 2AB
Tel: 01606 881 980

Hillingdon Independent Living, Wood End Centre, Judge Heath Lane, Hayes, Hillingdon, Middlesex UB3 2PB
Tel: 01895 484 880   Fax: 01895 484 882
Email: cnw-tr.hcfil@nhs.net
Web: www.hillingdoncentreforindependentliving.org.uk

William Merritt Disabled Living Centre and Mobility Service, St Mary's Hospital, Green Hill Road, Armley, Leeds LS12 3QE
Tel: 0113 350 8989   Fax: 0113 350 8681
Email: info@wmdlc.org   Web: www.wmdlc.org

British Red Cross Disabled Living Centre, 115, Clarendon Park Road, Leicester LE2 3AH
Tel: 0845 373 0217   Textphone: 0116 262 9465   Fax: 0845 373 0218
Email: dlcinfo@redcross.org.uk   Web: www.redcross.org.uk

Disabled Living Centre, Ancaster Day Centre, Boundary Street, Lincoln LN5 8NJ
Tel: 01522 545 111   Fax: 01522 545 111
Email: lincolndlc@redcross.org.uk   Web: www.redcross.org.uk

Disabled Living Foundation, Ground Floor, Landmark House, Hammersmith Bridge Road, London W6 9EJ
Tel: 0207 289 6111   Helpline: 0845 130 9177   Textphone: 0207 432 8009
Email: info@dlf.org.uk Fax: 0207 266 2922   Web: www.dlf.org.uk

British Red Cross Disabled Living Centre, Interagency Building, Stanley Avenue, Mablethorpe, Lincolnshire LN12 1DP
Tel: 01507 478574   Tel: 0845 0547171
Email: mablethorpeDLC@redcross.org.uk   Web: www.redcross.org.uk

Disabled Living Centre, Burrows House, 10, Priestley Road, Manchester M28 2LY
Tel: 0161 607 8200   Fax: 0161 607 8201
Email: info@disabledliving.co.uk   Web: www.disabledliving.co.uk

Independent Living Centre, Lansdowne Road, Middlesborough, Cleveland TS4 2PG
Tel: 01642 250 749   Fax: 01642 250 749   Text: 01642 244 718
Web: www.ilc.middlesborough.gov.uk

Milton Keynes Centre for Integrated Living, 330, Saxon Gate West, Central Milton Keynes, Buckinghamshire MK9 2ES
Tel: 01908 231 344   Text: 01908 231 505   Fax: 01908 231 335
Email: info@mkcil.org.uk

Northamptonshire Centre for Independent Living, Gladstone Road Resource Centre, Gladstone Road, Northampton NN5 7EJ
Tel: 01604 588 501   Cell phone: 07585 504 254   Fax: 01604 591 276
Web: Northamptonshire CIL

Disabilities Living Centre, Middleton Court, Glaisdale Parkway, off Glaisdale Drive, West Bilborough, Nottingham NG8 4GP
Tel: 0115 985 5780   Fax: 0115 928 4914
Email: info@dlcnotts.co.uk   Web: www.dlcnotts.co.uk

Guideposts Trust, Abingdon Resource and Wellbeing Centre, Audlett Drive, Abingdon, Oxfordshire OX14 3GD
Tel: 01993 899 985
Email: ilc@guidepoststrust.org.uk   Web: www.guidepostsilc.org.uk

Independent Living Centre, St George's Road, Semington, Wiltshire BA14 6JQ
Tel: 01380 871 007   Fax: 01380 871 113
Email:welcome.ilc.semington@googlemail.com   Web: www.ilc.org.uk

Disability Equipment Bradford, 103, Dockfield Road, Shipley BD18 4LQ
Tel: 01274 589 162   Fax: 01274 530 432
Email: equipment@disabilityadvice.org.uk   Web: Disability Advice

Disabled Living Centre, 33, Ryhall Road, Stamford, Lincolnshire PE9 IUF
Tel: 01780 480 599   Fax: 01780 480 603
Email: stamforddlc@redcross.org.uk   Web: www.redcross.org.uk

Unit 2b, Williamsport Way, Lion Barn Industrial Estate, Needham Market, Suffolk IP6 8RW
Tel: 01449 720809   Fax: 01449 723560
Email: info@agamobilitysystems.co.uk Web: www.agamobilitysystems.co.uk

Tremorvah Industries, Unit 8, Threemilestone Industrial Estate, Truro, Cornwall TR4 9LD
Tel: 01872 324 340   Text: 01872 324 364   Fax: 01872 324 372
Email: enquiries@tremorvah.cornwall.gov.uk   Web: www.tremorvah.co.uk

Hertfordshire Action on Disability, The Woodside Centre, The Commons, Welwyn Garden City AL7 4DD
Tel: 01707 324 581   Fax: 01707 371 297
Email: info@hadnet.org.uk   Web: www.hadnet.co.uk

East Cheshire Independent Living Centre, Dean Row Centre, Ringstead Road, Wilmslow, Cheshire SK9 2HA
Tel: 0300 123 5010 (option 3)

Neville Garratt Centre for Independent Living, Wolverhampton Social Services, Bell Street, Wolverhampton WVI 3PR
Tel: 01902 553648   Textphone: 01902 551 510
Email: ssces@wolverhampton.gov.uk

Organisations concerned with specific conditions

Action for ME (Myalgic Encephalomyelitis) ME Association, PO Box 2778, Bristol BS1 9DJ
Tel: 0117 927 9551   Tel: 0845 123 2380   Fax: 0117 927 9552
Email: 0117 930 7286   Web: www.actionforme.org.uk

Action on Hearing Loss (see under Royal National Institute for Deaf People)

Alzheimer's Society, Devon House, 58, St Katharine's Way, London EIW ILB
Tel: 020 7423 3500   Fax: 020 7423 3501
Email: enquries@alzheimers.org.uk   Web: www.alzheimers.org.uk

Anxiety UK, Zion Community Resource Centre, 339, Stretford Road, Hulme, Manchester M15 4ZY
Tel: 08444 775 774   Admin line: 0161 226 7727
Email: info@anxietyuk.org.uk   Web: www.anxietyuk.org.uk

Arthritis Care, Floor 4, Linen Court, 10, East Road, London N1 6AD
Tel: 020 7380 6500
Email: info@arthritiscare.org.uk   Web: www.arthritiscare.org.uk

Arthritis Action, 1, Upperton Gardens, Eastbourne, East Sussex BN21 2AA
Tel: 01323 416 550   Tel: 0800 652 3188
Email: info@arthriticassociation.org.uk Web: www.arthriticassociation.org.uk

Arthritis Research UK, Copeman House, St Mary's Court, St Mary's Gate, Chesterfield S41 7TD
Tel: 0300 790 0400   Fax: 0300 790 0401
Email: enquiries@arthritisresearchuk.org   Web: www.arthritisresearchuk.org

Asthma UK, Summit House, 70, Wilson Street, London EC2A 2DB
Tel: 0800 121 62 44   Web: www.asthma.org.uk

Ataxia UK, Lincoln House, Kennington Park, 1-3, Brixton Road, London SW9 6DE
Tel: 020 7582 1444   Helpline: 0845 644 0606
Email: helpline@ataxia.org.uk   Web: www.ataxia.org.uk

Backcare (previously the National Back Pain Association), 16, Elmtree Road, Teddington, Middlesex TW11 8ST
Tel: 020 8977 5474   Helpline: 0845 130 2704   Fax: 020 8943 5318
Email: info@backcare.org.uk   Web: www.backcare.org.uk

Bipolar UK (previously the Manic Depression Fellowship) (MDF), Victoria Charity Centre, 11, Belgrave Road, London SW1V 1RB
Tel: 020 7931 6480   Fax: 020 7931 6481
Email: info@bipolaruk.org.uk   Web: www.bipolaruk.org.uk

British Deaf Association (BDA), 2nd Floor, 356, Holloway Road, London N7 6PA
Tel: 0207 697 4140
Email: bda@bda.org.uk   Web: www.bda.org.uk

British Dyslexia Association, Unit 8, Bracknell Beeches, Old Bracknell Lane, Bracknell RG12 7BW
Tel: 0845 251 9003   Fax: 0845 251 9005
Email: admin@bdadyslexia.org.uk   Web: www.bdadyslexia.org.uk

British Heart Foundation, (BHF), Greater London House, 180, Hampstead Road, London NW1 7AW
Tel: 020 7554 0000   Textphone: 18001 020 7554 0000   Web: www.bhf.org.uk

British Institute of Learning Disabilities (BILD), Birmingham Research Park, 97, Vincent Drive, Edgbaston, Birmingham B15 2SQ
Tel: 0121 415 6960   Fax: 0121 415 6999
Email: enquiries@bild.org.uk   Web: www.bild.org.uk

The Limbless Veterans (previously the British Limbless Ex-Service Man's Association) (BLESMA), 185-187, High Road, Chadwell Heath, Romford, Essex RM6 6NA
Tel: 020 8590 1124   Fax: 020 8599 2932
Email: headquarters@blesma.org.   Web: www.blesma.org/

British Lung Foundation, 73-75, Goswell Road, London ECIV 7ER
Tel: 020 7688 5555   Helpline: 03000 030 555
Email: enquiries@blf.org.uk   Email: helpline@blf.org.uk
                    Web: www.blf.org.uk

The British Polio Fellowship, Eagle Point, The Runway, South Ruislip, Middlesex HA4 6SE
Tel: 0800 018 0586
Email: info@britishpolio.org.uk   Web: www.britishpolio.org.uk

The British Tinnitus Association (BTA), Ground Floor, Unit 5. Acorn Business Park, Woodseats Close, Sheffield S8 OTB
Tel; 0114 250 9922   Tel: 0144 250 9933   Helpline: 0800 018 0527
Minicom: 0114 258 5694   Fax: 0114 258 2279
Email: info@tinnitus.org.uk   Web: www.tinnitus.org.uk

Coeliac UK, 3rd Floor, Apollo Centre, Desborough Road, High Wycombe, Buckinghamshire HP11 2QW
Tel: 0845 305 2060   Web: www.coeliac.org.uk

Colostomy Association, Enterprise House, 95, London Street, Reading, Berkshire RG1 4QA
Tel: 0118 939 1537   Freephone: 0800 328 4257
Email: cass@colostomyassociation.org.uk
Web: www.colostomyassociation.org.uk

Continence Bladder and Bowel Foundation, SATRA Innovation Park, Rockingham Road, Kettering, Northants, NN16 9JH
Tel: 01536 533255   Helpline: 0845 345 0165
Web: www.bladderandbowelfoundation.org

Deafblind UK, National Centre for Deafblindness, John and Lucille van Geest Place, Cygnet Road, Hampton, Peterborough PE7 8FD
Textphone: 01733 358 100   Fax: 01733 358 356
Email: info@deafblind.org.uk   Web: www.deafblind.org.uk

Dementia Care Trust (DCT), Kingsley House, Greenbank Road, Easton, Bristol BS5 6HE
Tel: 0117 952 5325   Fax: 0117 951 8213   Web: www.dct.org.uk

Depression Alliance, 20, Great Dover Street, London SE1 4LX
Tel: 0845 123 23 20
Email: information@depressionalliance.org   Web: www.depressionalliance.org

Diabetes UK, Macleod House, 10, Parkway, London NW1 7AA
Tel: 0345 123 2399   Fax: 020 7424 1001
Email: info@diabetes.org.uk   Web: www.diabetes.org.uk

Down's Syndrome Association, Langdon Down Centre, 2a, Langdon Park, Teddington TW11 9PS
Tel: 0333 1212 300
Email: info@downs-syndrome.org.uk   Web: www.downs-syndrome.org.uk

Dyslexia Institute (National Training Office), Park House, Wick Road, Egham, Surrey TW20 OHH
Tel: 01784 222 300
Email: egham@dyslexiaaction.org.uk   Web: www.dyslexiaaction.org.uk

Dyspraxia Connexion, 21, Birchdale Avenue, Hucknall, Nottingham NG15 6DL
Helpline: 0115 9632220   Web: www.dysf.fsnet.co.uk

Epilepsy Action, New Anstey House, Gate Way Drive, Yeadon, Leeds LS19 7XY
Tel: 0113 210 8800
Email: epilepsy@epilepsy.org.uk   Web: www.epilepsy.org.uk

Epilepsy Society (previously National Society for Epilepsy) Chesham Lane, Chalfont St Peter, Buckinghamshire SL9 ORJ
Tel: 01494 601 300   Helpline: 01494 601 400
Web: www.epilepsysociety.org.uk

Headway – (the brain injury association), Bradbury House, 190, Bagnall Road, Old Basford, Nottingham NG6 8SF
Tel: 0115 924 0800   Helpline: 0808 800 2244   Fax: 0115 958 4446
Email: Email Headway

Hearing Link (previously Hearing Concern), 27-28, The Waterfront, Eastbourne, East Sussex BN23 5UZ
Tel: 0300 111 1113   SMS: 07526 123255   Fax: 01323 471 260
Email: enquiries@hearinglink.org   Web: www.hearinglink.org

The Limbless Association, Unit 16, Waterhouse Business Centre, 2, Cromar Way, Chelmsford, Essex CM1 2QE
Tels: 01245 216670/71/72   Helpline: 0800 644 0185
Email: enquiries@limbless-association/   Web: www.limbless-association.org

Macmillan Cancer Support, 89, Albert Embankment, London SE1 7UQ
Tel: 020 7840 7840   Freephone: 0808 808 0000   Fax: 020 7840 7841
Web: www.macmillan.org.uk

Marie Curie Cancer Care, 89, Albert Embankment, London SE1 7TP
Tel: 0800 716 146
Web: www.mariecurie.org.uk

Mencap, 123, Golden Lane, London EC1Y ORT
Tel: 020 7454 0454   Freephone: 0808 808 1111   Fax: 020 7608 3254
Email: help@mencap.org.uk   Web: www.mencap.org.uk

Mental Health Foundation, Colechurch House, 1, London Bridge Walk, London SE1 2SX
Tel: 020 7803 1100   Fax: 020 7803 1111   Web: www.mentalhealth.org.uk

Motor Neurone Disease Association, (MND), PO Box 246, Northampton NN1 2PR
Tel: 01604 250 505   Helpline: 08457 626262   Fax: 01604 624726/638289
Email: enquiries@mndassociation.org   Web: www.mndassociation.org

MS Society (Multiple Sclerosis Society), MS National Centre (MSNC) 372, Edgeware Road, London NW2 6ND
Admin: 020 8438 0700   Fax: 020 8438 0701
Email: infoteam@mssociety.org.uk   Web: www.mssociety.org.uk

Muscular Dystrophy Campaign, 61A, Great Suffolk Street. London SE1 OBU
Tel: 020 7803 4800
Email: info@muscular-dystrophy.org   Web: www.muscular-dystrophy.org

Mind (previously National Association for Mental Health), 15-19, Broadway, Stratford, London E15 4BQ
Tel: 020 8519 2122   Information line: 0845 766 0163   Fax: 020 8522 1725
Email: contact@mind.org.uk   Web: www.mind.org.uk

National Association of Deafened People (nadp), Dalton House, 60, Windsor Avenue, London SW19 2RR
Tel: 0845 055 9663 (message service)   Mobile(SMS only) 07527 211 348
Email: enquiries@nadp.org.uk   Web: www.nadp.org.uk

National Autistic Society, 393, City Road, London ECIV ING
Tel: 020 7833 2299   Helpline: 0808 800 4104   Fax: 020 7833 9666
Email: nas@nas.org.uk   Web: www.autism.org.uk

National Back Exchange, Linden Barns, Greens Norton Road, Towcester, Northamptonshire NN12 8AW
Tel: 01327 358855
Email: admin@nationalbackexchange.org
Web: www.nationalbackexchange.org

National Development Team for Inclusion (previously the National Development Team for People with Learning Difficulties,) First Floor, 30-32, Westgate Buildings, Bath BAI IEF
Tel: 01225 789135   Fax: 01225 338017
Email: office@ndti.org.uk   Web: www.ndti.org.uk

National Osteoporosis Society, Camerton, Bath BA2 OPJ
Tel: 01761 471771/0845 130 3076   Helpline: 0845 450 0230
Email: info@nos.org.uk   Web: www.nos.org.uk

Epilepsy Society (previously National Society for Epilepsy) Chesham Lane, Chalfont St Peter, Buckinghamshire SL9 ORJ
Tel: 01494 601 300   Helpline: 01494 601 400
Web: www.epilepsysociety.org.uk

No Panic, Jubilee House, 74, High Street, Madeley, Telford, Shropshire TF7 5AH
Tel: 01952 680 460   Helpline: 0800 138 8889
Email: admin@nopanic.org.uk   Web: www.nopanic.org.uk

Parkinson's Disease Society, 215, Vauxhall Bridge Road, London SWIV IEJ
Tel: 020 7931   Fax: 020 7233 9908
Email: hello@parkinsons.org.uk   Web: www.parkinsons.org.uk

The Partially Sighted Society, 1, Bennetthorpe, Doncaster, DN2 6AA
Tel: 0844 477 4966   Fax: 0844 477 4969
Email: reception@partsight.org.uk   Web: www.partsight.org.uk

Rethink (previously the National Schizophrenia Fellowship), Rethink Mental Illness,
89, Albert Embankment, London SE1 7TP
Tel: 0300 5000 927
Email: advice@rethink.org   Web: www.rethink.org

Royal National Institute of Blind People, RNIB Headquarters, 105, Judd Street,
London WCIH 9NE
Tel: 0303 123 9999   Email: helpline@rnib.org.uk   Web: www.rnib.org.uk

Action on Hearing Loss (previously the Royal National Institute for Deaf People)
(RNID), 19-23, Featherstone Street, London ECIY 8SL
Tel: 020 7296 8000   Textphone: 020 7296 8001 SMS 0780 0000 360
Freephones: 0808 808 0123   Textphone: 0808 808 9000   Fax: 020 7296 8199
Email: informationline@hearingloss.org.uk   Web: www.actiononhearingloss.org.uk

SANE, First Floor, Cityside House, 40, Adler Street, London E1 IEE
Tel: 020 7375 1002   Helpline: 0845 767 8000   Fax: 020 7375 2162
Email: info@sane.org.uk   Web: www.sane.org.uk

The Schizophrenia Association of Great Britain (SAGB), Web: www.sagb.co.uk

Scope, 6, Market Road, London N7 9PW
Tel: 020 7619 7100   Freephone: 0808 800 3333
Email: response@scope.org.uk   Web: www.scope.org.uk

SENSE (for deafblind people), 101, Pentonville Road, London N1 9LG
Tel: 0300 330 9256   Tel: 020 7520 0972
Textphones: 0300 330 9256/020 7520 0972
Email: info@sense.org.uk   Web: www.sense.org.uk

Speakability (Action for Dysphasic Adults), 240, City Road, London ECIV 2PR
Tel: 020 7261 9572   Helpline: 0808 808 9572
Email: speakability@speakability.org.uk   Web: www.speakability.org.uk

Spinal Injuries Association (sia), SIA House, 2, Trueman Place, Oldbrook, Milton
Keynes MK6 2HH
Tel: 0845 678 6633   Advice: 0800 980 0501   Fax: 0845 070 6911
Email: Email SIA here   Web: www.spinal.co.uk

Stroke Association, Stroke Association House, 240, City Road, London ECIV 2PR
Tel: 020 7566 0300   Helpline: 0303 303 3100
Textphone: 18001 0303 3033 100   Fax: 020 7490 2686
Email: info@stroke.org.uk   Web: www.stroke.org.uk

Terrance Higgins Trust, (HIV and AIDS charity), 314-320, Grays Inn Road, London
WCIX 8DP
Tel: 020 7812 1600   Fax: 020 7812 1601
Email: info@tht.org.uk   Web: www.tht.org.uk

Specialist organisations

Many of the societies previously listed, such as the Disabled Living Foundation,
provide advice, publications and equipment to help in daily living and specific activities.
The Societies listed below are each devoted to one particular subject:

Disabled Photographers Society, 37, Orchard Close. New Barn, Longfield, Kent
DA3 7JP
Web:disabledphotographers.co.uk

EXTEND (provides recreational exercise to music for the elderly and less able), 2,
Place Farm, Wheathampstead, Hertfordshire AL4 8SB
Tel: 01582 832760
Email: admin@extend.org.uk   Web: www.extend.org.uk

National Association of Flower Arrangement Societies (NAFAS), Osbourne House, 12, Devonshire Square, London EC2M 4TE
Tel: 020 7247 5567   Fax: 020 7247 7232
Email: flowers@nafas.org.uk   Web: www.nafas.org.uk

National Philatelic Society (stamp collecting), Freeling House, Phoenix Place, London WCIX ODL
Tel: 020 7239 2571
Email: nps@ukphilately.org.uk   Web:www.ukphilately.org.uk/nps/

Royal Society for the Protection of Birds (RSPB), The Lodge, Sandy, Bedfordshire SG19 2DL
Tel: 01767 680551
Email: enquiries@rspb.org.uk   Web: www.rspb.org.uk

Wheelchair Dance Association, 180, St Andrews Road South, St Anne's, Lytham, Lancashire FY8 1EU
Tel: 01253 722303/01253 725246   Fax: 01253 726040

First Aid

These organisations provide courses on First Aid: -

British Red Cross, UK Office, 44, Moorfields, London EC2Y 9AL
Tel: 0844 871 11 11   Textphone: 020 7562 2050   Fax: 020 7562 2000
Enquiries Tel: 08700 104950   Learn First Aid Tel: 0844 871 8000
Email: information@redcross.org.uk   Web: www.redcross.org.uk

St John Ambulance National Headquarters, 27, St John's Lane, London ECIM 4BU
Tel: 020 7324 4000   Fax: 020 7324 4001   Web: www.sja.org.uk

Access / mobility

Association of Train Operating Companies (ATOC), 2nd Floor, 200, Aldersgate Street, London ECIA 4HD
Tel: 020 7841 8000   Enquiries: 020 7841 8062

Email: customer.relations@nationalrail.co.uk   Web: www.nationalrail.co.uk
(The Association has a pamphlet 'Stations made easy' which gives details on how to
find information at the different stations using the National Rail Enquiries website: -
www.nationalrail.co.uk/stations_destinations/ – it also has a leaflet explaining the
Disabled Persons Railcard (A Senior Railcard is also available)

Automobile Association (AA customer support), Fanum House, Basingstoke,
Hampshire RG21 4EA
Tel: 0161 333 0752   Disability Helpline: 0800 262050
Email: email us form   Web: www.theaa.com
(The AA has a 'Disabled Travellers Guide' which gives information on all aspects of
travel with a car and also without one.)

Centre for Accessible Environments (cae) 4th Floor, Holyer House, 20-21, Red Lion
Court, London EC4A 3EB
Tel: 020 7822 8232   Fax: 020 7822 8261
Email: info@cae.org.uk   Web: www.cae.org.uk

Community Transport Association (CTA), Central Support Office, Highbank, Halton
Street, Hyde, Cheshire SK14 2NY
Tel: 0161 351 1475   Fax: 0161 351 7221
Email: info@ctauk.org   Web: www.ctauk.org
(The Community Transport Association runs training courses on the use of minibuses
for disabled people, they also have a newsletter and publications)

Department for Transport (DfT) (see Government Departments) Blue Badge Scheme
(This scheme allows disabled people to park in certain areas which are not permitted
to other drivers. Details about the scheme can be found in the booklet 'The Blue Badge
Scheme – parking concessions for disabled and blind people' which is available when
the blue badge is being supplied.
Tel: 0844 463 0213
Email: bluebadge@northgate-is.com   Web: www.gov.uk/apply-blue-badge

Forum of Mobility Centres, 2, Napier Place, Thetford, Norfolk IP24 3RL
Tel: 01842 824657
Email: mobility@rcht.cornwall.nhs.uk   Web: www.mobility-centres.org.uk
Letters to: – c/o, Providence Chapel, Warehorne, Ashford, Kent TN26 2JX
Tel: 0800 559 3636

(This service gives advice to disabled drivers and passengers on suitable types of vehicles and adaptations and has access to various publications for disabled people).

Motability Operations, 22, Southwark Bridge Road, London SE1 9HB
Tel: 0300 456 4566
Web: www.motability.co.uk

The National Federation of Shopmobility UK (NFSUK), 163, West Street. Fareham, Hampshire PO16 OEF
Tel: 0844 41 41 850
Email: Info@shopmobilityuk.org   Web: www.shopmobilityuk.org

National Key Scheme (NKS), Disability Rights UK, 12, City Forum, 250, City Road, London ECIV 8AF
Tel: 020 7250 3222
Email: enquiries@disabilityrightsuk.org   Web: www.radar-shop.org.uk
(The National Key Scheme enables disabled people to use toilets for the disabled which are otherwise locked. A key is available from Disability Rights UK or the Local Authority. There is also a book 'National Key Scheme – Accessible Toilets for Disabled People.'

Transport for London, tfl Customer Services, 4th Floor, 14, Pier Walk, London SE10 OES
Tel: 0343 222 1234   Textphone: 08001 123 456   Web: tfl.gov.uk

Dial-a-ride, Passenger Services, PO Box 68799, London SEIP 4RD
Tel: 0343 222 7777   Textphone: 18001–020 7309 8900   Fax: 0207 394 5218
Email: DAR@tfl.gov.uk

TRIPSCOPE, The Vassall Centre, Gill Avenue, Bristol BS16 2QQ
Tel: 0117 939 7783   Helpline: 08457 58 56 41   Fax: 0117 939 7736
Email: enquiries@tripscope.org.uk   Web: www.rvi.org.uk/tripscope.htm
(Tripscope gives travel advice and transport information for the elderly and people who are disabled or have difficulty in getting around)

Holidays / travel

Disability Rights UK, (previously RADAR), 12, City Forum, 250, City Road, London ECIV 8AF

Tel: 020 7250 3222

Email: enquiries@disbilityrightsuk.org   Web: www.radar-shop.org.uk

(Disability Rights have a handbook and guide for disabled people wanting to go on holiday, they also have other information for anyone wanting to travel.)

English Heritage, 1, Waterhouse Square, 138-142, Holborn, London ECIN 2ST

Tel: 020 7973 3000 /0870 333 1181   Minicom text: 0800 015 0516

Fax: 020 7973 3001

Email: customers@english-heritage.org.uk   Web: www.english-heritage.org.uk

(English Heritage have a guide 'The English Heritage Guide' for visitors with disabilities)

Holiday Care (Holidays for the Disabled), 8, Honeybourne Way, Orpington, Kent BR5 IEZ

Tel: 08448 117 558   Web: www.holiday-care.co.uk

Information about rail travel   Tel: 08457 48 49 50

Email: customer.relations@nationalrail.co.uk Web: www.nationalrail.co.uk

(railcards are available for young people (16-25yrs), family and friends, the disabled and the elderly)

Information about travel in London on the buses and underground, Customer Services, 4th Floor, 14, Pier Walk, London SE10 OES

Tel: 0343 222 1234   Textphone: 08001 123 456   Web: tfl.gov.uk

The National Trust, PO Box 574, Manvers, Rotherham S63 3FH

Tel: 0844 800 1895   Fax: 0844 800 4642

Email: enquiries@nationaltrust.org.uk   Web: www.nationaltrust.org.uk

(The National Trust has a booklet 'Information for Visitors with Disabilities)

The Ramblers Association, 2nd Floor, Camelford House, 87-90, Albert Embankment, London SE1 7TW

Tel: 020 7339 8500   Fax: 020 7339 8501

Email: ramblers@ramblers.org.uk   Web: ramblers.org.uk

Web: (disabled ramblers) www.disabledramblers.co.uk

Vitalise Centres (short breaks/holidays), Short Break Bookings Team, 212, Business Design Centre, 52, Upper Street, London N1 OQH

Tel: 0303 303 0145   Fax: 0207 288 6899

Email: bookings@vitalise.org.uk   Web: www.vitalise.org.uk

Support Dogs

Canine Partners National Training Centre, Mill Lane, Heyshott, Midhurst, West Sussex GU29 OED
Tel: 08456 580 480   Web: www.caninepartners.org.uk

Guide Dogs for the Blind Association, Burghfield Common, Reading RG7 3YG
Tel: 0118 983 5555   Fax: 0118 983 5433
Email: guidedogs@guidedogs.org.uk   Web: www.guidedogs.org.uk

Hearing Dogs for Deaf People, The Grange, Wycombe Road, Saunderton, Princes Risborough, Buckinghamshire HP27 9NS
Tel: (voice and Minicom): 01844 348 100   Fax: 01844 348 101
Email: info@hearingdogs.org.uk   Web: www.hearingdogs.org.uk
Support Dogs, 21, Jessops Riverside, Brightside Lane, Sheffield S9 2RX
Tel: 0114 261 7800   Fax: 0114 261 7555
Email: info@supportdogs.org.uk   Web: www.support-dogs.org.uk

Pets

The Cinnamon Trust, 10, Market Square, Hayle, Cornwall TR27 4HE
Tel: 01736 757900   Fax: 01736 757010
Email: admin@cinnamon.org.uk   Web: www.cinnamon.org.uk
(The Cinnamon Trust gives support to elderly people who may need assistance in looking after their pet.

Pets as Therapy Ltd. 14A, High Street, Wendover, Buckinghamshire HP22 6EA
Email: reception@petsastherapy.org

Leisure activities

The following organisations have different activities covering arts, crafts and games. Some also have aids to make these easier.

The Ability Superstore, PO Box 1099, Colne BB9 4DU
Tel: 0161 85 00 88 4/0800 255 0498
Email: heretohelp@abilitysuperstore.com   Web: www.abilitysuperstore.com

Anything Left-handed, Sterling House, 18, Avenue Road, Belmont, Surrey SM2 6JD
Tel: 020 8770 3722   Fax: 020 8715 1220
Email: enquiries@anythingleft-handed.co.uk
Web: www.anythinglefthanded.co.uk
(They have a range of items for anyone who may be left-handed and also publications)

Artsline, c/o 21, Pine Court, Wood Lodge Gardens, Bromley BR1 2WA
Email: ceo@artsline.org.uk   Web: www.artsline.org.uk

British Jigsaw Puzzle Library, Clarendon, Parsonage Road, Herne Bay, Kent
CT6 5TA
Tel: 01227 742222
Email: jigsawinfo@aol.com   Web: www.britishjigsawpuzzlelibrary.co.uk
(This library also has semi-interlocking and non-interlocking jigsaws)

British Red Cross Ability Mail Order, 113, Clarendon Park Road, Leicester LE2 3AH
Tel: 01162 449049   Fax: 01162 745979
Web: www.redcross.org.uk

Coats Crafts UK, Green Lane Mill, Holmfirth HD9 2DX
Tel: 01484 681881
Email: consumer.ccuk@coats.com   Web: www.coatscrafts.co.uk
(This firm has embroidery and tapestry kits – their mail order retailer is Stitchability
(see over page)

Disabled Living Foundation, Ground Floor, Landmark House, Hammersmith Bridge
Road, London W6 9EJ
Tel: 020 7289 6111   Helpline: 0300 999 0004
Email: info@dlf.org.uk   Web: www.dlf.org.uk
(The Disabled Living Foundation gives advice and has information on leisure activities
and suppliers)

DMC Creative World Ltd, Unit 21, Warren Park Way, Warrens Park, Enderby, Leicester
LE19 4SA
Tel: 0116 275 4000   Web: www.dmccreative.co.uk
(DMC have a catalogue giving details about their needlework kits)

The Jigsaw Gallery Ltd, Unit 23, Level 1, St Nicholas Centre, St Nicholas Way, Sutton, Surrey SM1 1AW
Tel: 020 8661 7597   Fax: 020 8661 7597
Email: sales@jigsawgallery.com
(The Jigsaw Gallery has an online service)

John Jacques Ltd, House of Jacques, 1, Fircroft Way, Edenbridge, Kent TN8 6EL
Tel: 01732 500200   Fax: 01732 500111   Web: www.jaqueslondon.co.uk
(John Jacques Ltd have a selection of quality games including solitaire, noughts and crosses, bagatelle, backgammon and a cribbage board)

Keep Able, 3/4, Sterling Park, Pedmore Road, Brierley Hill, West Midlands DY5 1TB
Tel: 0800 085 0688
Email: homeshopping@keepable.co.uk   Web: www.keepable.co.uk

Knitwell Wools Ltd, (Jean Greenhowe's Designs), 116, Sunbridge Road, Bradford BD1 2NF
Tel: 01274 722290   Fax: 01274 393564   Web: knitwell.co.uk
(Knitted doll patterns)

La Hacienda Ltd, Hangar 27, Site C, Aston Down Airfield, Nr. Stroud, Gloucestershire GL6 8HR
Tel: 01285 762060   Fax: 01285 760746
(La Hacienda supply games e.g. skittles, noughts and crosses, lawn darts, giant chess/draughts etc.)

Mattel UK Ltd, Mattel House, Vanwall Business Park, Vanwall Road, Maidenhead, Berkshire SL6 4UB
Tel: 01628 500303   Web: www.service.mattel.com/uk
(Mattel have a selection of Scrabble games available through their retailers.)

Nottingham Rehab Supplies (NRS), Ceva House, Excelsior Road, Ashby-de-la-Zouch, Leicestershire LE65 ING
Tel: 0845 121 8111
Email: customerservice@nrs-uk.co.uk   Web: www.nrs-uk.co.uk
(Nottingham Rehab Supplies have a wide range of games and other activities)

Oasis Art and Craft Products Ltd, Goldthorne Road, Kidderminster, Worcestershire DY11 7JN
Tel: 01562 744522   Web: www.reeves-art.com
(Oasis have a selection of art and craft materials)

Readicut, Ashford, Kent TN24 OZX
Tel: 0844 858 9311   Tel (orders): 0844 858 9320
Email: Customercare@readicut.co.uk   Web: www.readicut.co.uk
(Readicut have a selection of rugmaking kits)

Royal National Institute of Blind People (RNIB), RNIB Headquarters, 105, Judd Street, London WCIH 9NE
Tel: 0303 123 9999
Email: helpline@rnib.org.uk   Web: www.rnib.org.uk
(The RNIB have a selection of activities for the visually impaired)

Smitcraft, Unit 1, Eastern Road, Aldershot, Hampshire GU12 4TE
Tel: 01252 342626
Email: info@smitcraft.com   Web: www.smitcraft.com
(Smitcraft have a variety of crafts and a selection of jigsaws and playing cards, they also have carpet bowls, croquet and skittles)

Specialist Crafts Ltd, Hamilton House, Mountain Road, Hamilton, Leicester LE4 9HQ
Tel: 0116 269 7711   Fax: 0116 269 7722   Web: www.specialistcrafts.co.uk
(Specialist Crafts have a wide range of materials)

Stitchability Web: www.stitchability.co.uk

Winslow Resources, Goyt Side Road, Chesterfield, Derbyshire S40 2PH
Tel: 01246 210416
Email:hello@winslowresources.com   Web: www.winslowresources.com
(Winslow have a selection of different activities in their catalogue – these include quizzes, reminiscence and games. They also have publications)

Gardening

Gardening for Disabled Trust, PO Box 285, Tunbridge Wells, Kent TN2 9JD
Web: www.gardeningfordisabledtrust.org.uk
(The Gardening for Disabled Trust gives out grants for tools and equipment and to make gardens easier for disabled people. It also produces a magazine and has information on aids and techniques)

Thrive (formerly Horticultural Therapy), The Geoffrey Udall Centre, Beech Hill, Reading RG7 2AT
Tel: 0118 988 5688   Fax: 0118 988 5677
Email: Thrive's Information Service   Web: www.thrive.org.uk
Thrive runs several garden projects and also supports other projects where gardening is used for training, employment, therapy and health. It gives advice to elderly and disabled people and does research into the benefits of gardening)

The following firms supply tools and equipment, which may be used by people who are elderly or disabled: -

B&Q Customer Services, Catesby Business Park, White Rose Way, Doncaster DN4 8DG
Tel: 0845 609 6688   Email: diy.com   Web: www.diy.com
(B&Q have a range of products with a 'Daily Living Made Easier' symbol for the elderly and disabled – they also have an online service)

Betterware has an online shop   Web: www.betterware.co.uk
(They supply a long-handled weeding knife, a set of tools with interchangeable handles and a long-handled cultivator, which has different heads)

Fiskars Brands Inc, Customer Care Team, 2537, Daniels Street, Madison, W1 53718, USA
Tel: 1(866) 342-5661   Web: www.fiskarsbrands.com
(Fiskars have a selection of different kinds of gardening tools)

Peta (UK) Ltd, Charles House, Park Farm, Kelvedon Road, Inworth, Colchester CO5 9SH
Tel: 01376 573 476   Fax: 01376 570 023
Email: custserv@peta-uk.com
(Peta have long handled tools with adapted handles – they also make scissors, knives etc.)

Spear and Jackson, customer Service, Atlas Way, Atlas North, Sheffield S4 7QQ
Tel: 0114 281 4242   Fax: 0114 281 4252
Email: sales@spear-and-jackson.com   Web: spearandjacksongroup.com

Reading

Audible Ltd, Colet Court, 100, Hammersmith Road, London W6 7JP
Tel: 0800 496 2455
Email: customercare@audible.co.uk   Web: www.audible.co.uk
(Audible have a range of books etc., which can be downloaded and played back on personal computers, CD's or AudibleReady computer based mobile devices)

Audiobooks (BBC), BBC Shop, Technicolour Unit A, Cosford Lane, Newbold, Rugby CV21 IQN
Tel: 0844 846 1417
Email: bbcshop@bbc.com   Web: www.bbcshop.com
(BBC Audiobooks have a wide range of books on tape and compact disc)

National Library for the Blind, Far Cromwell Road, Stockport, Cheshire SK6 2SG
Tel: 0161 355 2094   Fax: 0161 355 2098
                              Web: www.nlb-online.org
(The National Library for the Blind has tactile books and music in braille. It also produces a journal.)

Readers Digest, Vivat Direct (t / a Readers Digest), 4th Floor, 57, Broadwick Street, London WIF 9QS
Tel: 0845 601 2711   Customer Services: 0871 351 1000
Email: customer-service@readersdigest.co.uk   Web: www.readersdigest.co.uk

Readers Digest (Large print)   Web: www.ask.com/Readers+Digest+Large+Print

Royal National Institute for the Blind (RNIB) audio book service, RNIB Headquarters, 105, Judd Street, London WCIH 9NE
Tel: 0303 123 9999
Email: helpline@rnib.org.uk   Web: rnib,org.uk

National Talking Newspapers and Magazines (TNAUK), National Recording Centre, Heathfield, East Sussex TN21 8DB

Tel: 01435 866102   Fax: 01435 865422
Email: info@tnauk.org.uk   Web: www.tnauk.org.uk
(The Talking Newspaper Association has a wide range of newspapers and magazines in different forms e.g. tape, disk, email etc)

Ulverscroft Large Print Books Ltd, The Green, Bradgate Road, Anstey, Leicester LE7 7FU
Tel: 0116 236 4325   Fax: 0116 234 0205
Email: sales@ulverscroft.co.uk   Web: www.ulverscroft.co.uk
(Ulverscroft have a large selection of large print books and audio books)

Music

Music in Hospitals, Case House, 85-89, High Street, Walton-on-Thames, KT12 IDZ
Tel: 01932 260810   Fax: 01932 224123
Email: info@music-in-hospitals.org.uk   Web: www.musicinhospitals.org.uk
(Music in Hospitals also gives concerts in hospices, nursing and residential homes and day centres)
National Library for the Blind has music in braille (see previous page)

The Partially Sighted Society, 1, Bennetthorpe, Doncaster, DN2 6AA
Tel: 0844 477 4966   Fax: 0844 477 4969
Email: reception@partsight.org.uk   Web: www.partsight.org.uk
(The Partially Sighted Society has a small book of popular carols in large print)

Soundsense
Email: info@soundsense.org   Web: www.soundsense.org
(The National Music and Disability Information Service can be found at Soundsense)

Ulverscroft Large Print Books Ltd, The Green, Bradgate Road, Anstey, Leicester LE7 7FU
Tel: 0116 236 4325   Fax: 0116 234 0205
Email: sales@ulverscroft.co.uk   Web: www.ulverscroft.co.uk
(Ulverscroft have song books in large print)

Winslow Resources, Goyt Side Road, Chesterfield, Derbyshire S40 2PH
Tel: 01246 210416
Email: hello@winslowresources.com   Web: www.winslowresources.com
(Winslow have CDs and DVDs which can be used with older people)

Miscellaneous

Able 2 Wear, 53, Donaldson Street, Kirkintilloch, Glasgow G66 IXG
Tel: 0141 7753738
Email: info@able2wear.co.uk   Web: www.able2wear.co.uk
(clothing for the disabled including those using a wheelchair)

NHS Direct,
Tel: 111   Web: www.nhsdirect.nhs.uk

Royal Society for the Prevention of Accidents (ROSPA), ROSPA House, 28, Calthorpe
Road, Edgbaston, Birmingham B15 IRP
Tel: 0121 248 2000   Fax: 0121 248 2001
Email: help@rospa.com   Web: www.rospa.com

The Stationery Office, (TSO), 85, Buckingham Gate, London SWIE 6PD
Tel: 0870 600 5522
Email: customer.services@tso.co.uk   Web: www.tsoshop.co.uk

Specialist Publishers

Age Exchange, Reminiscence Centre, 11, Blackheath Village, London SE3 9LA
Tel: 020 8318 9105
Email: administrator@age-exchange.org.uk   Web: www.age-exchange.org.uk

Age UK publications, Tavis House, 1-6, Tavistock Square, London WCIH 9NA
Tel: 0800 169 6565   Web: www.ageuk.org.uk/publications
(Age UK have a range of publications and factsheets for the elderly)

EBIS (HSE), The Coach House, Harestone Hill, Caterham, Surrey CR3 6DH
Tel: 0845 5195347   Fax: 0845 5195473
Email: info@ebis-hse.com   Web: www.ebis-hse.com
(EBIS have a selection of Health and Safety booklets, which can be used with the
elderly and disabled)

Hawker Publications Ltd, Culvert House, Culvert Road, London SW11 5DH
Tel: 020 7720 2108 (Ext. 211)   Fax: 020 7498 3023
Email: remi@hawkerpublications.com   Web: www.careinfo.org/books/

Jessica Kingsley Publishers, 73, Collier Street, London N1 9BE
Tel: 020 7833 2307   Fax: 020 7837 2917
Email: hello@jkp.com   Web: www.jkp.com

Royal National Institute of Blind People (RNIB), PO Box 173, Peterborough, Cambs PE2 6WS
Tel: 0303 123 9999   Fax: 01733 375001
Email: shop@rnib.org.uk   Web: www.rnib.org.uk
(The RNIB publishes magazines, catalogues and other books for blind and partially sighted people)

Search Press Ltd, Wellwood, North Farm Road, Tunbridge Wells, Kent TN2 3DR
Tel: 01892 510850   Fax: 01892 515903
Email: searchpress@searchpress.com
(Search Press produce books on arts, crafts and leisure)

Speechmark Publishing Ltd, Unit C5, Sunningdale House, 43, Caldecotte Lake Drive, Caldecotte Lake Business Park, Milton Keynes, MK7 8LF
Tel: 01908 277 177   Fax: 01908 278 297
Email: customer.services@speechmark.net   Web: www.speechmark.net
(Speechmark have a wide range of books on the care of the elderly and different disorders – they also have games and activities which can be done with the elderly)

Winslow Resources, Goyt Side Road, Chesterfield, Derbyshire S40 2PH
Tel: 01246 210416
Email: hello@winslowresources.com   Web: www.winslowresources.com
(Winslow Resources have games and activities which can be used with the elderly and also a large selection of publications)

FURTHER READING

Catalogues

Homecraft Rolyan, Nunn Brook Road, Huthwaite, Sutton in Ashfield, Nottinghamshire NG17 2HU
Tel: 08444 124 330   Fax: 08448 730 100
Email: homecraft.sales@patterson-medical.com   Web: www.homecraft-rolyan.com
(Homecraft Rolyan have a wide range of mobility aids and also some games)

NRS Healthcare, Sherwood House, Cartwright Way, Forest Business Park, Bardon Hill, Coalville, Leics, LE67 1UB
Tel: 0845 121 8111   Fax: 0845 121 8112
Email: customerservice@nrs-uk.co.uk   Web: www.nrs-uk.co.uk
(Nottingham Rehab Supplies have a wide range of products including aids, equipment, recreational activities, crafts etc)

RNIB (The Royal National Institute for the Blind) 105, Judd Street, London WCIH 9NE
Tel: 020 7388 1266   Helpline: 0303 123 9999   Fax: 020 7388 2034
Email: helpline@rnib.org.uk   Web: www.rnib.org.uk

RNIB (Orders, enquiries and customer services), PO Box 173, Peterborough PE2 6WS
Tel: 0303 123 9999/01733 375350   Minicom: 0845 758 5691
Fax: 01733 37 50 01
Email: shop@rnib.org.uk   Online shop: www.rnib.org.uk/shop
(The RNIB have a selection of booklets giving information about the different aids which can be used by the blind and partially sighted, these include one on 'Games, toys and leisure')

Winslow, Goyt Side Road, Chesterfield, Derbyshire S40 2PH
Tel: 0845 230 2777   Fax: 01246 551195
Email: sales@winslow-cat.com   Web: www.winslow-cat.com
(Winslow have a wide range of books and games and also items which can be used for reminiscence)

Lifestyle

'Brighter Futures' Kidlington, T. Kitwood, S. Buckland, T. Petie, Anchor Housing Association
'Fit for the Future: a new vision for older people's care and support' Counsel and Care
'The Future of Homecare: responding to older people's needs' Counsel and Care and Ceretas
'Lifelong: a new vision for the wellbeing of all older people, their families and carers' Counsel and Care
'Lifestyle Matters' Claire Craig, Gail Mountain, Speechmark

Care Homes

'All About Me – residents express their views' NAPA (National Association for Providers of Activities for Older People)

'Ascertaining wishes: a good practice guide – advance care planning for care homes for older people' Counsel and Care

'The Brief Care Home Guide' Counsel and Care

'Campaigning for Quality Care in Care Homes' Counsel and Care

'Care Home Handbook' (this book gives advice about choosing a care home and funding care). Counsel and care

'Care Homes in the Heart of the Community' (Final report of the NAPA Growing with Age Project) S. Knocker, B. Avila. NAPA

'Choice of Accommodation – care homes' Age UK

'The Complete Care Home Guide' Counsel and Care

Finding care home accommodation' Age UK

'How to Make Your Care Home Fun' K. Agar. Jessica Kingsley

'The human rights of Residents in Care Homes' Relatives and Residents Association

'I have Come to Visit' B. Koschland. Relatives and Residents Association

'Moving stories: The impact of admission into a care home on residents' partners' A. Clarke, L. Bright. Relatives and Residents Association

'On Being the Relative of Someone in a Home' D. White. Relatives and Residents Association

'Showing restraint: challenging the use of restraint in care homes' Counsel and Care

'Your care home – is it up to standard? Counsel and Care

Finances

'A Charter for Change' (concerning the gap in care-funding) Counsel and Care

'Finding and financing care in hard times' Counsel and Care

'Getting legal advice' Age UK

'NHS continuing healthcare and NHS-funded nursing care' Age UK

'Paying for care in a care home if you have a partner' Age UK

'Paying for temporary care in a care home' Age UK

'Paying for permanent residential care' Age UK

Volunteers

'The Good Practice Guide' Volunteering England

'Involving Relatives and Friends: A good practice guide for homes for older people' J. Burton-Jones. Relatives and Residents Association

'A Relative's Perspective: The need to involve relatives and friends' D. White. Relatives and Residents Association

'Volunteers in Care Homes for Older People: An underused opportunity' Rose Heatley. Relatives and Residents Association.

Dementia

'The Alzheimer's Society Book of Activities' S. Knocker NAPA

'Best practice in Design for People with Dementia' Dementia Services Development Centre, University of Stirling

'Celebrating the Person – Activity Pack' C. Craig. Dementia Services Development Centre, University of Stirling

'Challenging Behaviour in Dementia' G. Stokes. Speechmark

'Enriched Care Planning for people with Dementia' H. May, P. Edwards, D. Brooker. Jessica Kingsley

'The Essential Dementia Care Handbook' G. Stokes, F. Goudie. Speechmark

'Getting Everyone Included – Report of a research project involving people with dementia in a creative arts project' Magic Me (www.magicme.co.uk)

'Journal of Dementia Care' publishes articles relating to creative activities with people with dementia' Hawker Publications

'Living with Dementia' C. J. Gilleard. Croom Helm

'Person-Centred Dementia Care' D. Brooker. Jessica Kingsley

'The Source for Alzheimer's and Dementia' P. Britton Reese (available from Winslow)

'Therapeutic Activities with persons disabled by Alzheimer's Disease and related disorders' C. Bowlby (available from Winslow)

'Well Being in Dementia: An Occupational Approach for Therapists and Carers' T. Perrin, H. May. Churchill Livingstone

Visual Impairment

'How to guide people with sight problems' RNIB

The In Touch Handbook: Services for people with a visual handicap. BBC Publications.

Planning activities

'Care Homes in the Heart of the Community' B. Avila, S. Knocker. NAPA
'Closing the care gap' Counsel and Care.
'Developing Team Spirit and Co-operation – A guide for activity providers.' NAPA
'Functional Performance Record' NAPA
(A record to help in the assessment of Daily living skills)
'The Group Leader's Toolkit' R. Dynes. Speechmark
'Local Resources booklet' NAPA
'The Pool Activity Level (PAL) Instrument for Occupational Profiling: a practical resource for carers of people with dementia' J. Pool. Jessica Kingsley
'Rights, Risk and Restraint-Free Care of Older People, R. Hughes. Jessica Kingsley
'Safeguarding older people from abuse' Age UK
'Starting Out and Keeping It Up – A guide for activity providers' NAPA
'The Successful Activity Co-ordinator: A Learning Resource for Activity and Care Staff Engaged in Developing an Active Care Home' R. Hurtley, J.Wenborn. Age UK
'Training Manual for Working with Older People in Residential and Day Care Settings' J. Pritchard (available from Winslow)

Groupwork / activities

'Activities Encyclopaedia – 535 Best Activity Ideas' M. Knoth. Winslow
'Activities for Adults with Learning Disabilities' H. Sonnet, A. Taylor. Jessica Kingsley
'Activities of Daily Living Planner' NAPA
'Activity Allsorts' NAPA
'Activity Planning at Your Fingertips – (All the Activities You'll Ever Need) M. Knoth. Winslow
'The Activity Year Book – A Week by Week Guide for Use in Elderly Day and Residential Care' A. Bowden, N. Lewthwaite. Jessica Kingsley
'Breath of Fresh Air' NAPA
(Activities which can be done outside)
'The Classic Quiz Book' R. Dynes. Speechmark
'Communication Activities with Adults' J. Comins, F. Llewellyn, J. Offiler. Speechmark
'Creative Games in Groupwork' R. Dynes. Speechmark
'Creative Groupwork with Elderly People – Drama' M. Anderson-Warren. Speechmark

'Creative Themes for Groupwork and Personal Development'
S. Pinn-Atkinson, J. Woolloff. Speechmark
'Group Activities with Older Adults' V. Dent. Speechmark
'Groupwork Activities' D. Walsh. Speechmark
'The Groupwork Manual' A. Hickson. Speechmark
'Learning and Leisure' Age UK
'Memory Games for Groups' R. Dynes. Speechmark
'The New Culture of Therapeutic Activity with Older People' T. Perrin. Speechmark
'The Non-Competitive Activity Book' R. Dynes. Speechmark
'Not only Bingo – a study of good practice in providing recreation and leisure activities
    for older people in residential and nursing homes' Counsel and Care
'Quiz Book for Groups-Famous People' T. Payne. Speechmark
'Therapeutic Activities for Older People in Care Settings: A Guide in Good Practice'
T. Perrin (NAPA)
'Therapeutic Groupwork for People with Cognitive Losses'
M. Bender. Speechmark

Manual handling

'Basic Back Care' Backcare
'Carers Guide to Safer Handling of People' Backcare
'Guide to the Handling of People' Backcare
'Handling of People' National Back Exchange
'Managing your back' Backcare
'Manual handling assessments in hospital and in the community:
an RCN guide'
'Safer Handling of people in the Community' Backcare
'Standards in Manual Handling' National Back Exchange

Exercise

'Creative Movement and Dance in Groupwork' H. Payne. Speechmark
'Exercise for Older People – Training Pack' NAPA
'Gentle Exercises and Movement for Frail People' M. Hook. Speechmark
'More than Movement for Fit to Frail Older Adults – Creative Activities for the Body,
    Mind and Spirit' P. Postiloff Fisher. Health Professions Press
'You Can Do It – Exercises for Older People' M. Ruddlesden. Hawker Publications

Music

'And Still the Music Plays' G. Stokes. Hawker Publications
'As Time Goes By' (Unit 4, Albert Street, Droylsden, Manchester M43 7BA.
Tel: 0161 3706908
(Nostalgic music)
'Creative Music in Groupwork' C. Achenbach. Speechmark
'Invitation to the Dance: dance for people with dementia and their carers' H. Hill.
    Dementia Services Development Centre, University of Stirling
'Music and memories' (Good Music Record Co. Hay's House, PO Box 261, St Austell,
    Cornwall PL25 9EH.
Tel: 01726 819111   Web: www.goodmusic.co.uk)
(Nostalgic music and videos)
'Music Therapy in Dementia Care' D. Aldridge. Jessica Kingsley
'Responding to Music' M. Mullan, J. Killick. Dementia Services Development Centre,
    University of Stirling
'Song Book – Words for 100 popular songs' Speechmark
(There is a singalong tape to accompany some of the songs in this book)
'Song Books' – in large print and singalong tapes. Winslow

Reminiscence

'The Reminiscence Handbook – Ideas for Creative Activities with Older People'
C. Osborn. P, Schweitzer. Age Exchange
'Reminiscence in Dementia Care' P. Schweitzer. Age Exchange
'The Reminiscence Puzzle Book' R, Dynes. Speechmark
'The Reminiscence Quiz Book' M. Sherman. Speechmark
'The Reminiscence Skills Training Handbook' A. Rainbow. Speechmark
'Reminiscence – Social and Creative Activities with Older People in Care'
R. Sim. Speechmark
'Reminiscing with People with Dementia – A Handbook for Carers'
E. Bruce, S. Hodgson, P. Schweitzer. Age Exchange

Leisure

'The Art Activity Manual – A groupwork resource' M. Cropley. Speechmark
'Celebrating the Person: A practical approach to art activities' C. Craig.
Dementia Services Development Centre, University of Stirling.

'Creative Art in Groupwork' J. Campbell. Speechmark

'Creative Drama in Groupwork' S. Jennings. Speechmark

'Creative Games in Groupwork' R. Dynes. Speechmark

'Creative Themes for Groupwork and Personal Development'
S. Pinn-Atkinson, J, Woolloff. Speechmark

'Crochet Unravelled' Anything Left-handed (for people wanting to crochet left-
handed)

'Gardening is for Everyone' A. Cloet, C. Underhill. Thrive

'Gardening in Homes: A guide for relatives in nursing and residential care homes'
P. Hutchence. Relatives and Residents Association.

'Leisure activities' Disabled Living Foundation.

(A factsheet issued by the Disabled Living Foundation)

'No Cook Cooking' NAPA

'Storymaking and Creative Groupwork with Older People' P. Crimmens.
Jessica Kingsley

'The Woven Thread – activities in residential care' S. Gaspar. NAPA

'Write on – a book about creative writing' NAPA

Travel

'Access for Disabled Visitors' Historic Scotland

'Access to air travel – Guidance for disabled and less mobile passengers' – Disabled
Persons Transport Advisory Committee

'Care in the Air – advice for disabled travellers' Air Transport users Council

'Design Specification for On-Board Wheelchair for commercial passenger aircraft'
DPTAC

'Door to Door – A guide to transport for Disabled People' RADAR

'Essential Minibus Driving' Dring and Collins. ROSPA

'Flying High' Disabled Living Foundation

'Guidance on the Safe Transportation of Wheelchairs' Medical Devices Agency.

'Guidance on the safe Use of Wheelchairs and Vehicle-mounted Passenger Lifts'
Medical Devices Agency

'Guide for People with Disabilities' English Heritage

'Guide for the Disabled Traveller' Automobile Association

'Holidays in Britain and Ireland: A Guide for Disabled People' RADAR

'Information about Trust Properties for Disabled Visitors' The National Trust for
Scotland.

'Information for Visitors with Disabilities' The National Trust

'National Key Scheme Guide – Accessible Toilets for Disabled People' RADAR
'Rail Travel made easy' available from rail stations.
'The Rough Guide to Accessible Britain' Motability
(This book can be ordered on line at www.accessibleguide.co.uk
or by telephone 0800 953 7070)
'The Traintaxi Guide' available from W.H.Smith or www.traintaxi.co.uk
'Travelling with Assistance Dogs in Taxis and Private Hire Vehicles – Advice for
    disabled people' Department of Transport
'Your rights to fly – A step by step guide for disabled and less mobile passengers'
    Department of Transport

(For information about publications from the Community Transport Association see
    www.ctauk.co.uk)

Other Activities

Daily Telegraph Cryptic Crosswords. Collections published every six months. Pan Books.
Daily Telegraph Quick Crosswords. Collections published every six months. Pan Books
Jumbo Print Crossword Book. Terry Pitts-Fenby. Age Concern Grub Street.
Quiz Books. Winslow

Miscellaneous

'Choosing pressure relief equipment' Disabled Living Foundation
'Clothing ideas for Wheelchair users' Disabled Living Foundation
'Out and About with your Wheelchair' Disabled Living Foundation
First Aid Manual. St. John Ambulance/St Andrews Ambulance/British Red Cross.

Leaflets

Many of the organisations listed under Elderly, Disability and Specific Conditions have
    information leaflets on a wide range of subjects. They will provide lists if required.

Videos, CDs and Tapes

Winslow have a selection of videos, CDs and tapes in their 'Health and Rehabilitation'
    catalogue which can be used for reminiscence and singing.

REFERENCES

'Able to Garden' P. Please, Batsford

'A Field Guide to the Birds of Britain and Europe' Collins

'All Expenses Paid' The Volunteer Centre

'An Outline of Geriatrics' H.M Hodgkinson, Academic Press

'Assisting a Wheelchair User' Scriptographic Publications

Booklets on crochet and embroidery. J & P Coats

'Caring for Elderly People' Susan Hooker. Routledge & Kegan Paul

'Centre Active' Age Concern, Scotland

'Centre Forward' Age Concern, Scotland

'Creative Games in Groupwork' R. Dynes. Speechmark

'Choosing a wheelchair' RADAR

'Directory for Older People' Ann Darnborough & Derek Kinrade,
Woodhead-Faulkner

'Gardening in Retirement' Isobel Pays, Age Concern

'Gardening Time' William Davidson, Tiger Books

'General Guidance for Hearing Aid Users' HMSO

'The Gentle Art of Listening: Counselling skills for volunteers' Janet K. Ford, &
        Philippa Merriman, Volunteer Centre

'Getting the Best from your Wheelchair' RADAR

'Giving Good care – An introductory guide for care assistants' Help the Aged

'Groupwork Activities' D. Walsh. Speechmark

'Growing Indoor Plants' Ronald Menage, Ward Lock

'Hints on the use of your wheelchair' Department of Health

'How to coach Blind Bowlers' The English National Association of Visually
        Handicapped Bowlers.

'How to push a wheelchair' Disabled Motorist's Club

'How to start Bowling' Cotswold Bowls Centre

'Hypothermia' British gas plc

'Incontinence' Nicholas Laboratories, Slough

'Know the Game: Billiards and Snooker' A & C. Black

'Know the Game: Chess' A & C. Black

'Know the Game: Patience Games' A & C. Black

'Left-Handers Guide to Knitting' Anything Left-Handed Ltd.

'Minibus Drivers Handbook' Community Transport Association

'Official Handbook' British Crown Green Bowling Association

'Protecting Volunteers' The Volunteer Centre

'Rail Travel for Disabled Passengers'

'Rule Book' English Short Mat Bowling Association

'Supporting Volunteers' Mark Rankin, Volunteer Centre

'The Bird Table Book' Tony Soper, David and Charles

'The Essential Dementia Care Handbook' G. Stokes, F. Goudie. Speechmark

'The Good Practice Guide to Therapeutic Activities with Older People in Care
    Settings' T. Perrin. Speechmark

'The New Book of Patience Games' Ruth D. Botterill, W. Foulsham

'The New Culture of Therapeutic Activity with Older People' T. Perrin. Speechmark

'The Practice of Occupational Therapy' Ann Turner, Churchill Livingstone

'Wheelchair Owners Manual' Everest and Jennings

'Wheelchairs' (5th edition), The Disability Information Trust.